THE COUNTRY HOUSE

D1103255

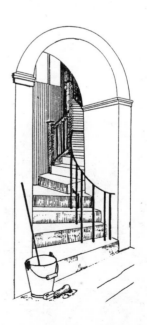

HOW IT WORKED

Peter Eric Lambourne

MCMXXX - MCMXC

·DONA·EUM·REQUIEM·

FISHING LODGE

Also by John Vince: 'Old Farms', 'Power Before Steam'.

THE
COUNTRY HOUSE
~HOW IT WORKED

JOHN VINCE

JOHN MURRAY

Text & illustrations © John Vince 1991
First published in 1991
by John Murray (Publishers) Ltd
50 Albemarle Street, London W1X 4BD

British Library Cataloguing in Publication Data
Vince, John 1932~
    The workings of the country house.
    1. English household equipment, history
    I. Title
    683.8
    ISBN 0-7195-4769-5

Printed in England by Clays Ltd., St Ives plc

CONTENTS

INTRODUCTION

The COUNTRY HOUSE was not an isolated part of rural society, but the focus of an elaborate community that embraced the FAMILY, its indoor and outdoor servants, as well as the adjacent village & farms. It was not unusual for the ESTATE to own all the land in a village. The century following Queen Anne's Coronation in 1702 was one of relatively rapid change in many aspects of English life brought about by stability & growing agricultural & commercial prosperity. Vast areas of countryside were altered by ENCLOSURES which banished the OPEN FIELDS & substituted the patchwork of irregular-shaped fields with hedgerows. This is a pattern that has been reversed only in the last thirty years.

Two significant improvements took place in communications. Better roads were paid for by tolls levied by Turnpike Trusts ~ post 1730. The development of the canal system made the transportation of goods much easier. Some of the wealth generated by an expanding commerce & industry found its way into the architectural improvements of the country house & its surrounding landscape. Houses were rebuilt or built from new & the surrounding parklands re-shaped by men such as Kent, Campbell, Paine, Carr, Adam & Capability Brown. Sometimes a complete village was moved ~ like Milton Abbas, Dorset ~ to allow a new 'view' to be created.

BEFORE the C18, furniture was made from the native timber ~ oak & elm; & from the 1660s walnut. In the Georgian period tropical hardwoods like mahogany & satinwood began to appear, the heavier styles were replaced by new designs of great elegance & a mechanical element was sometimes introduced.

The new, or remodelled, houses took on a different aspect. No longer was the mediaeval hall the focus of a family's life. Daily routine was enacted in several rooms; dining rooms, libraries, drawing rooms ~ saloons ~ all became part of this new design for living. Windows & window panes were bigger, letting in more light. Smaller rooms could be heated more effectively, especially with the help of new cast-iron coal ~ burning grates. Lighting was by candles until the oil lamp was introduced in Victorian days. No doubt women's influence was behind many of these developments.

This book is concerned particularly with the hidden workings, & various devices which helped to run that intricate equation - THE COUNTRY HOUSE - above & below stairs, inside & outside, in the stable block, gardens & in the park.

THE SERVANTS' WING

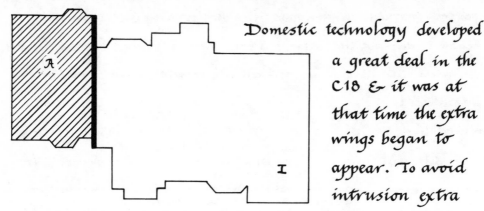

Domestic technology developed a great deal in the C18 & it was at that time the extra wings began to appear. To avoid intrusion extra premises were erected on the colder northern side of a house. To keep them in greater obscurity hedges, often of laurel, were grown about them; thus adding to the gloom.

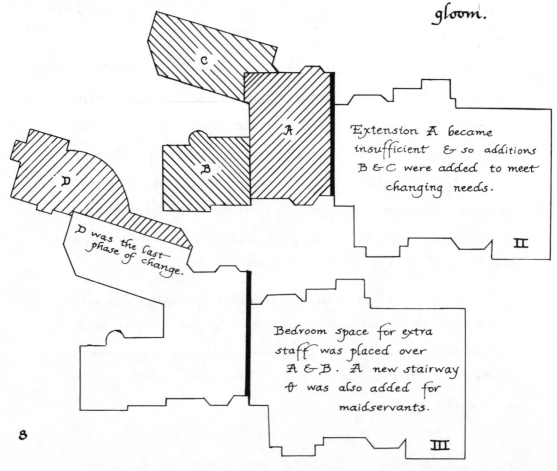

Extension A became insufficient & so additions B & C were added to meet changing needs.

D was the last phase of change.

Bedroom space for extra staff was placed over A & B. A new stairway was also added for maidservants.

Diagram I shows how a service wing started as a rectangular addition to the original house shape. When it was first built the new wing [A] was considered large enough to fulfil all the work it would be expected to perform. In time the techniques of cooking changed & more demands were made on laundry services. Clothes were changed & washed more often – thus more space & staff were needed.

This plan shows how the dining room linked the house & the service wing. This was common ground for the family & house servants. You can see how the additions eventually made up a long winding passage. Where a bit-by-bit development of this kind took place the location of the kitchen probably changed several times.

The principal rooms are numbered 1 – VII.

KEY TO PLAN ~ 1 Bakery : 2 Store : 3 Lamps : 4 & 5 Larders : 6 Scullery : 7 Boot Room : 8 Laundry 9 Kitchen : 10 Brush Room : 11 Butler's Bedroom : 12 Butler's Pantry : 13 Servants' Hall : 14 Still Room : 15 Housekeeper : 16 Office : Σ Male stairs : ɱ Luggage .

THE HOUSEHOLD

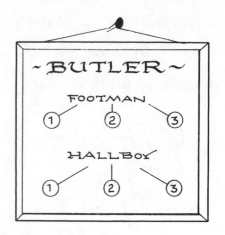

Within the household to serve the family there were three sub-divisions of indoor staff which are outlined here. There was a definite hierarchy which operated below stairs & its traditions were rigidly observed. The Butler, Housekeeper, footmen & housemaids [& a governess or nurse if such were employed] had business to take them into the realm of the gentry. Most of the staff, however long they worked in the house, never saw the inside of the dining room or trod the wide main staircase. A country house employed a large number of servants ~ some as many as fifty, but there were houses which had as few as ten. In a very large house there was sometimes a STEWARD who was at the top of the domestic pyramid, but the BUTLER was usually the male figurehead below stairs.

HOUSEKEEPER

HOUSEMAID

① ② ③

DUKE

BED 7

The servants were graded in a strict pecking order. They shared meals in the servants' hall but very often the senior servants, [cook, housekeeper & butler] withdrew to consume their dessert in the privacy of the housekeeper's room. The lower servants were entitled to a dessert on ~perhaps~ three days a week. Waste of any kind was deplored & many kitchens had emblazoned on their walls the slogan ~ ·WASTE NOT · WANT NOT ·

·RVLES ··· TO·BE·OBSERVED·HERE·

That every Servant must~
Take off his Hat at Entering
Sit in his proper Place at Table
Keep himself clean becoming his Station
Drink in his Turn
Be diligent in his Business
Shut the Door after him

That no Servant be guilty of ~
Cursing or Swearing
Speaking disrespectfully of any one
Telling Tales
Breeding any Quarrel
Wasting Meat or Drink
Intermeddling with any other's Business
Unless requested to Afirst

The person offending to be deprived his Allowance of Beer - for the first Offence 3 Days
Second offence one whole week - and third Offence - his behaviour to be laid before
Mr. Myddleton.

HEARTHS

OPEN HEARTH

A FIREBACK & protected the masonry at the base of the chimney. Pots could be raised or lowered with a pot hook or chain. Most had tripod feet so they could stand firmly among the embers:~ e.g. the SKILLET [B]. Fire could be placed in a RAISED BASKET[C] which rested on FIRE DOGS [D]. A BREAD OVEN [E] was often built into the fireplace wall. The SALT BOX [F] was always placed close to the fire to keep its contents dry. SPIT JACKS [G] were placed above the mantleshelf & their weights [H] hung at the side. Curtains [J] on a rail helped the fire to draw when closed. A rack for bacon [K] was to be found in most kitchens. The SPIT RACK [L] was another common feature.

THE RAISED HEARTH was a development of the Open Hearth. A low oven could be built into its structure. This was heated from above & below as the diagram

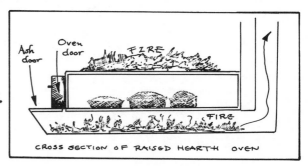

Ash door

Oven door

FIRE

FIRE

CROSS SECTION OF RAISED HEARTH OVEN

shows. Ashes were removed via the ash door when the bottom fire had gone out.

THE TABLE-TOP STOVE seems to have been introduced in the C18. Working at a higher level must

have been easier for the cooks. This brick-built stove has a cast-iron top. Each section has a removable lid so that pots can be exposed to the fire's full heat. Its upper corners are stone which does not distort like bricks in intense heat. Iron straps support the brickwork. The fire is supported on bars (x) & ash removed at (y). Many utensils could be heated to different temperatures all at the same time on a stove of this kind.

PORTABLE CLOAM OVENS, MADE OF CLAY, WERE WIDELY USED FROM THE C17 ONWARDS.

13

OVENS & RANGES

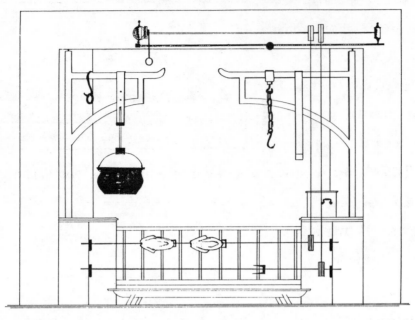

The space inside an OPEN HEARTH was often filled in with a basket grate. This allowed two chimney cranes to be fitted as the above example shows. Space at the side was often built up to provide a warming place for pots. The raised fire was still used to roast meat on the spits. A long drip tray stood on the floor below. In the C19 the HASTENER allowed meat to be held vertically - it was turned by a CLOCK JACK [*η*]. The hastener stood before the fire. Its shape reflected and retained the heat.

SOME BASKET GRATES HAD AN OVEN OR A HOT WATER TANK AT THE SIDE.

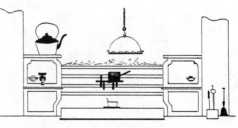

14

HASTENER

One disadvantage of the basket grate was its length & the amount of fuel it consumed. In the mid~C19 the cast iron range was introduced. Early examples had an oven at the side

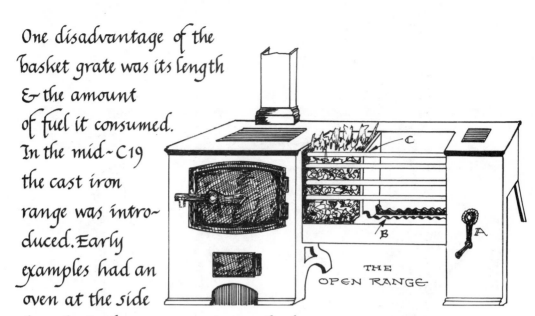

THE OPEN RANGE

but the basket grate remained. There was an important refinement however which made it possible to alter the size of the fire. This was achieved by a handle [A] that turned a spur gear. The spur gear moved a rack [B] which in turn changed the position of the fire~plate [C]. Open ranges allowed fuel to be used more economically.

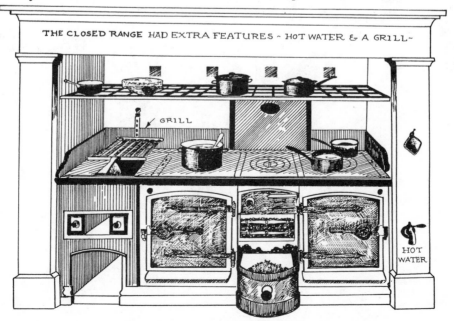

THE CLOSED RANGE HAD EXTRA FEATURES ~ HOT WATER & A GRILL~

GRILL

HOT WATER

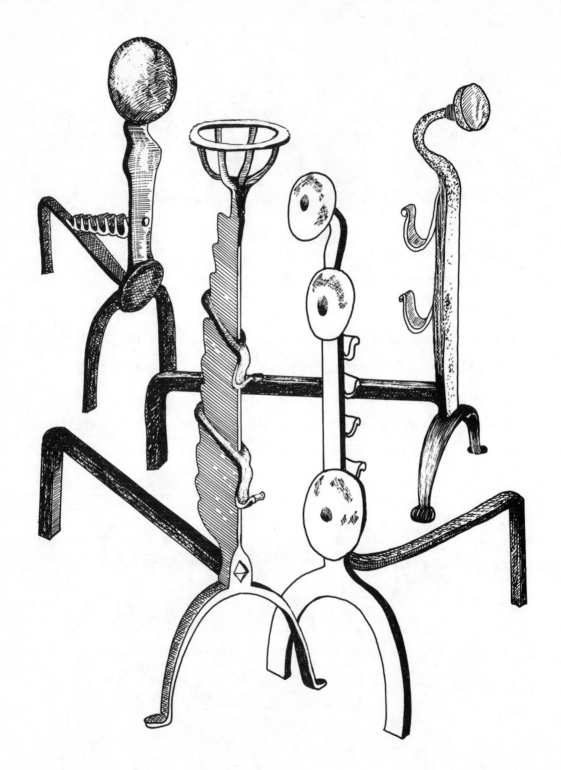

DOGS & SPITS

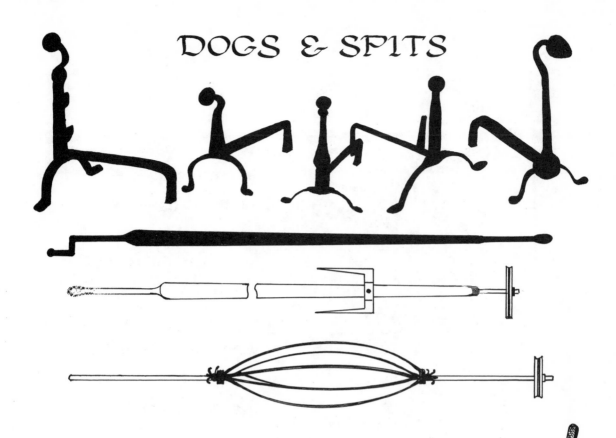

One of the most arduous tasks before the invention of spit jacks & smoke jacks was turning the spit, a hot & sticky job that was usually given to a kitchen boy. Most of the fireside furniture was made by the blacksmith & very durable. The spit dogs shown opposite allowed a spit to be placed at different levels ~ according to the strength or size of the fire. One of these looks like a chimney hook & has supports for two spits. At the top there is a cup-shaped cresset which could hold a candlestick or a basting vessel.

17

SPIT JACK

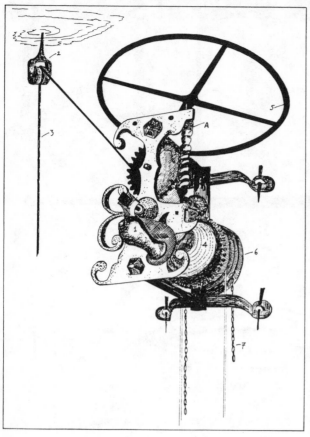

It is uncertain when an anonymous genius made the connection between weight driven clocks and the need to rotate a spit to roast a dinner. Blacksmiths were our early technicians but they were also artists and any examination of the frontplate of a spit~jack will reveal carefully fashioned curves. This example from the C17 shows a crowned figure holding a shafted weapon in each hand. The initials & date show it to be a one-off creation.

One of the interesting features of the spitjack is the worm gear (A) which connects the flywheel to the third spurwheel, also found in the smoke jack on page 20.

To operate the spitjack the weight was wound up ~ like a clock ~ with the handle in front of the faceplate (1). A pulley (2), or sometimes two, was used to keep the weight clear of the fireplace. When the weight was raised the cord (3) was wound around the barrel (4). The motion began when the flywheel (5) was rotated. Then the weight began to descend. Two or three pullies (6) at the back of the winding spindle could be used to operate the spits in front of the fire. Sometimes a fine chain (7) was used for this purpose as it was more resistant to heat. The spit (8) was supported by spit dogs (9) which could hold two or three spits in different positions. A drip tray (10) was placed below to catch the hot fat.

WEIGHT

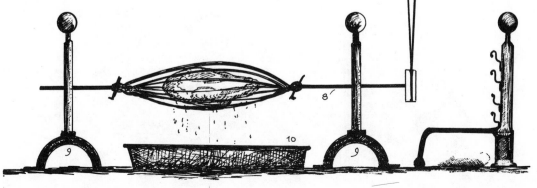

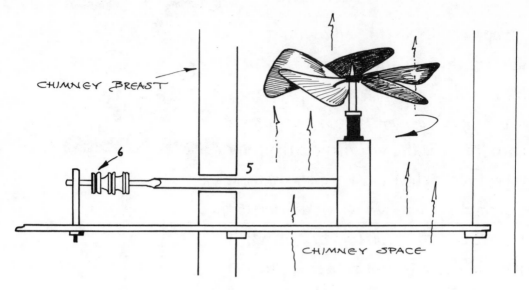

CHIMNEY BREAST

6

5

CHIMNEY SPACE

SMOKE JACK

One of the mechanical marvels of the C17 or thereabouts was the device which enabled the spit to be rotated by the rising warm air in the chimney. It is interesting to see the way in which the blacksmith constructed the jack. The blades of the fan [1] were set at an angle. This allowed the air to push the blades as it ascended. How the originators knew the best way to arrange the blades we can only guess, but the same principle was employed by the Saxons & Vikings on their watermills: see my POWER BEFORE STEAM.

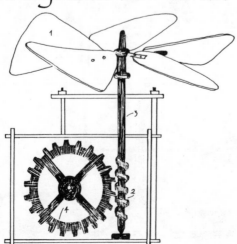

The second feature of interest is
the WORM GEAR [2] on the fan
spindle. This is made of iron and
the profile of the screw-like curve
was no doubt finished with a file. Each
rotation of the spindle [3] moved a tooth
on the spur gear [4], but at a slow rate.
It was the low gearing of the device
which made it workable. Before
the spiral WORM GEAR was made
in iron examples in wood had been
fashioned. So it was that the black~
smith borrowed ideas from the carpenter. The spur gear spindle [5] protruded
through the chimney wall & presented

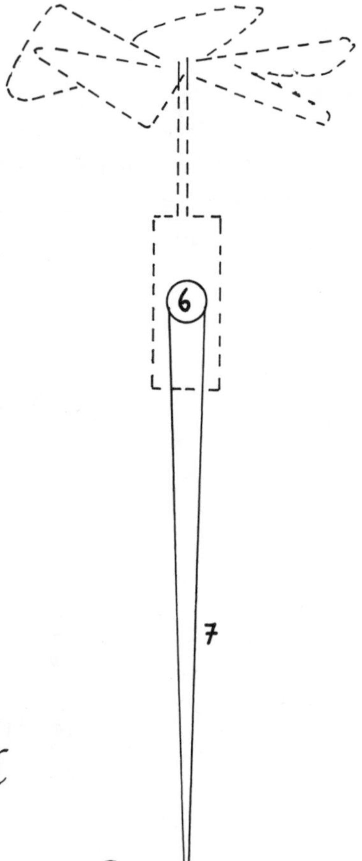

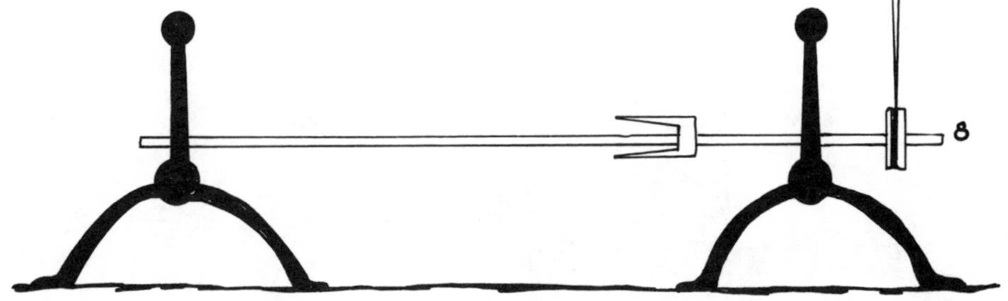

pullies [6] for the cook to use. The diagram above shows
the cook's view of the spit & the smoke jack hidden in the
chimney. As the pulley [6] rotated its motion was translated
through 90° to operate the spit [8] by way of the
twisted driving cord [7].

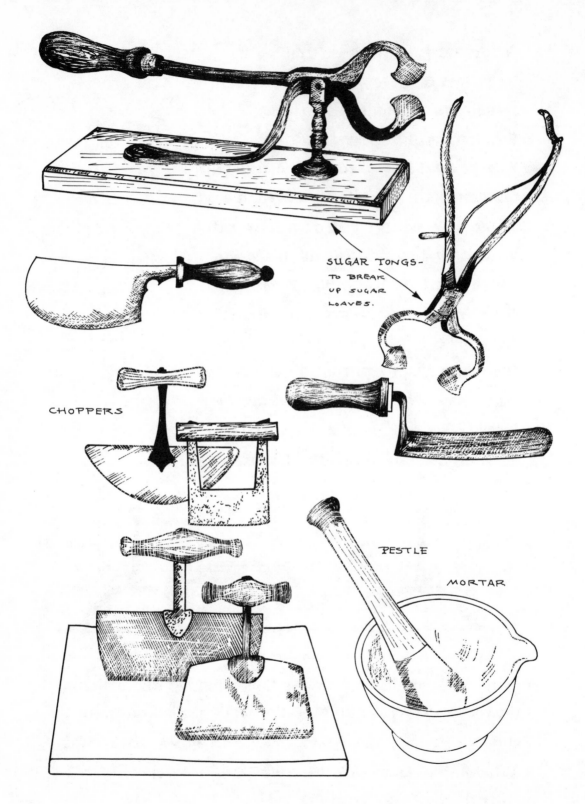

SUGAR TONGS-
TO BREAK
UP SUGAR
LOAVES.

CHOPPERS

PESTLE

MORTAR

22

KITCHEN TOOLS

When preserved or prepared products first appeared they were treated with contempt by the experienced cook. The tools most often used in prepackaged days were simple & had a long ancestry. Ingredients that were not chopped up were ground down. In large kitchens there would probably be one very heavy chopping block made of a solid piece of beechwood. Mortars too could be made in the solid, & some had a guide for the pestle. Tedious hours were spent on such work by the kitchen maids. The process of preserving food in a vacuum-sealed container was invented, in 1795, by a Frenchman Louis Appert. Tin cans were introduced in 1812, but the first tin opener was made in the 1860s!

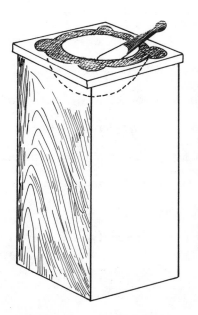

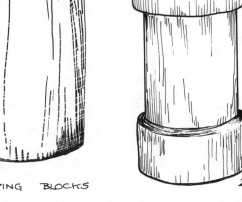

CHOPPING BLOCKS

This mid-C19 print of a kitchen shows that every cook made use of a great number of tools. The gas lighting indicates how up-to-date the kitchen really is ~ even though the meat is cooking on a clock jack in front of a basket grate. There are no windows ~ a roof light provides illumination.

The tools shown are : A~ Tin openers which were invented in the 1850s, a long time after canned food was introduced in 1812. B~ Plate warming cabinet with sliding doors at the front. C~ Colander for straining vegetables ~ made in clay, brass & enamel ware. D~ Candle-powered food warmer. E~ Pie cup. F~ Plum-shaped ice mould to decorate desserts. G~ Enamel grid iron, fat was collected at x. H~ Wooden pestle & mortar for herbs. I~ Adjustable toaster to hook to fire bars.

A

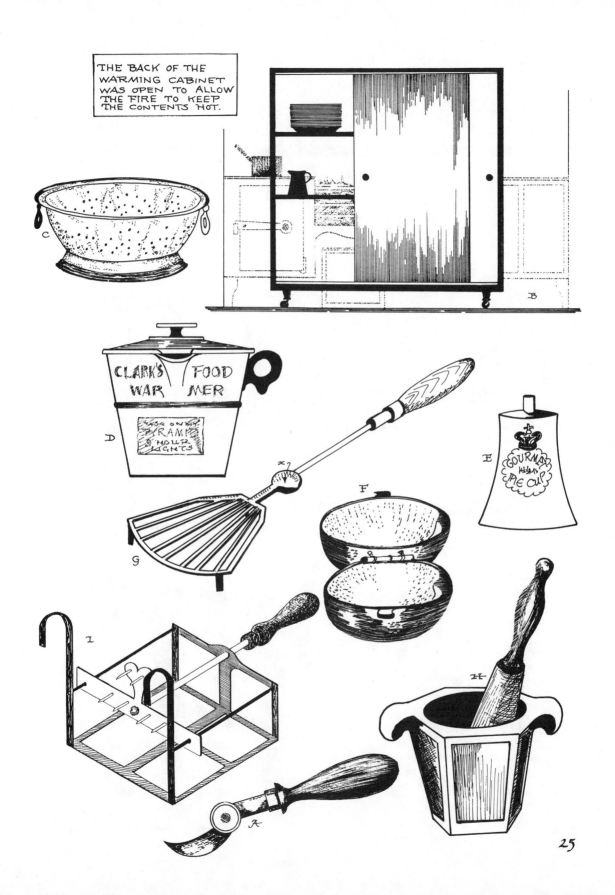

THE BACK OF THE
WARMING CABINET
WAS OPEN TO ALLOW
THE FIRE TO KEEP
THE CONTENTS HOT.

25

STRETCHERS
ROTTED AWAY
ON RUSH
FLOORS.

AH 1713

26

KITCHEN SEATS

Even overworked kitchen staff were
sometimes allowed to sit down. When
floors were rush strewn & the rushes
changed at infrequent intervals joint
stools were used. Surviving examples
often show wear & damage where the
feet stood among soggy rushes. A few such stools bear a
date. On uneven floors a three-legged stool was more stable
~a fact well known to milkmaids. The form of chair with a
solid seat which provided an anchor for legs & the superstruc-
ture is usually called a WINDSOR CHAIR. This type of
chair was made in the Chilterns,
but seats of the same type were made
in all parts of the country. The common-
est kitchen chair in the C19 was probably
the plain scroll back Windsor chair
made in High Wycombe. In the Servants'
Hall the Butler or Housekeeper
would occupy an arm chair;
but the remaining staff sat
upon plainer single chairs,
or benches & settles.

27

THE BUTLER'S PANTRY

SAFE

WORKTOP
WINE CARRIER

BUTLER'S TRAY & STAND

The care of the family silver was the Butler's responsibility. Once cleaned it was stored in the Butler's Pantry & inside the silver safe. This had an imposing secure door, protecting a walk-in cupboard with its baize-covered shelves. Larger objects, like soup tureens, were kept wrapped in baize bags. In some houses the Butler or a footman slept close to the pantry with a blunderbuss to hand, to guard the plate. Strongroom doors were skilfully engineered & usually bear a maker's plate like the one shown here.

DOORPLATE

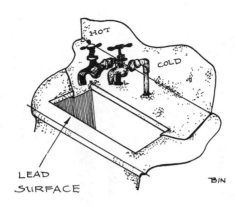

HOT

COLD

LEAD
SURFACE

1815
E.I.
MALMSEY

CYDER

VERY
OLD. PORT.

BIN LABELS

PERRY

It was important to label bins & decanters correctly, & an efficient Butler had to be familiar with a wide range of wines. The bin labels in the cellar were made of metal or pottery, but the labels used on decanters in the dining room were silver or silver plated. Decanter labels have chains so they can hang round the necks of their respective vessels.

In older houses wooden sinks remained RAISIN in use long after stoneware became common. The wooden sinks often had a lead lining to prevent warping. A hot water supply was a much later addition to piped water. Taps were frequently odd as a result.

DECANTER
LABEL

SHRUB

BASKET-WORK BOTTLE
CARRIER

BOTTLE
TRAY

29

BRASS STUDS

THE GREEN BAIZE DOOR

c. 1790

BUTLER'S TRAY TABLE

The boundary between the servants' wing & the house was marked by a green baize door. Most of the servants never stepped beyond it. The door's thickness helped to protect the house from the noise of domestic bustle.

The tray-table was designed to provide a resting place for the portable tray. Examples may also have been used in the dining room. Such workaday items are now valued by collectors of antique furniture.

BELOW. Left — coal scuttle. Right — Decanting Machine, usually mahogany & brass.

THE WARMING ROOM

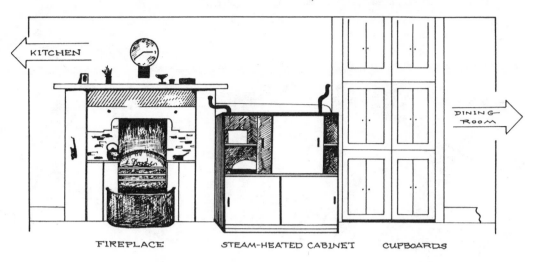

KITCHEN

DINING ROOM

FIREPLACE   STEAM-HEATED CABINET   CUPBOARDS

The kitchen was usually a long way from the dining room & food could get cold in transit. In the C19 it became common for a WARMING ROOM to be placed next to the dining room. This had a fire & often a cabinet heated by hot water pipes. The Butler supervised much of the work which had to be performed here & in the warming room various items peculiar to his office could be found ~ viz. the BUTLER'S TRAY.

The decanting machine, very suitable for crusted wines which 'threw' a big sediment, had a screw mechanism which could tilt a bottle with great precision. This allowed the sediment, or lees, to remain in the bottle & not to be transferred to the decanter. Sieved funnels were also used.

CORKSCREWS

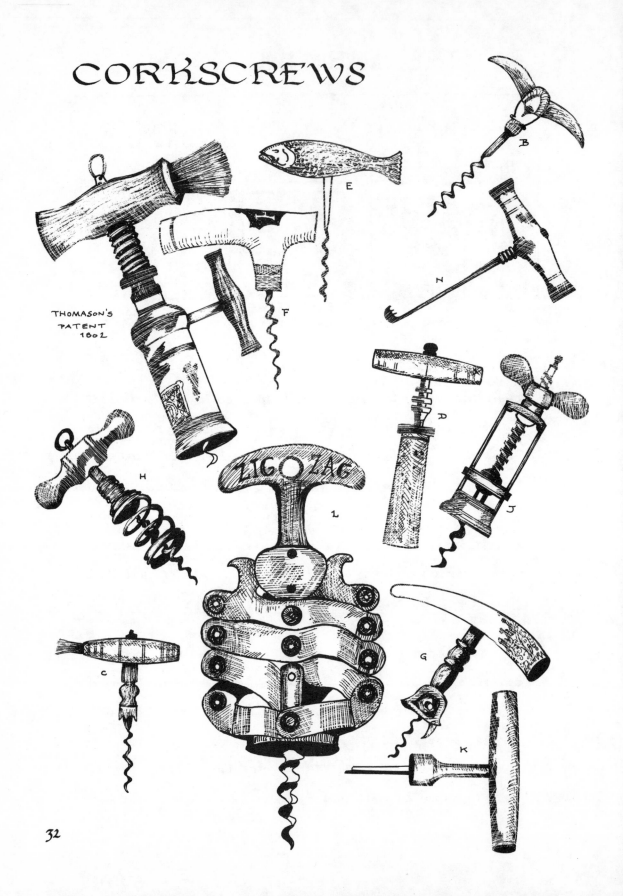

THOMASON'S
PATENT
1802

ZIG ZAG

A great deal of ingenuity was applied to the task of removing corks from bottles. Part of the vast gallery of designs is shown here. Quite complicated mechanics were eventually introduced using rack & pinion gears~ they were miniature versions of cart jacks used by wheelwrights. The concept is at least as old as Leonardo da Vinci. In the C18 brushes were added to handles so that fragments of the wax seal or mould could be removed before opening.

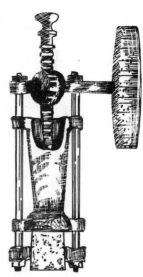

RACK & PINION TYPE
C19

A. Georgian Button Type corkscrew in ivory. Its serrated button helped to grip the cork.
B. Bull's horn design in silver.
C Georgian type with cork grip & brush.
D. French-style screw in ivory and brush. E. The silver fish was a popular design. Its screw was made of steel. F. A corkscrew which also served as the top of a walking stick. G. This device was also a bottle opener. H. A spring~loaded screw with a wooden grip. J. An early (c.1799) screw thread with an elegant winged nut. K. The 'Butler's Friend' which allowed the cork to be withdrawn without trace! L. A robust corkscrew which could expand trellis~fashion, levering against the bottle top. M. The double lever type which is still made today. N. A cork extractor for use on 'lost' corks. P. An unusual combination instrument ~ a corkscrew, foil cutter & tongs.

THOMAS LUND'S   BOTTLE GRIP 1838

KNIFE CLEANING

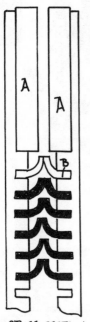

Before stainless steel was invented ~ c. 1914 ~ the business of knife cleaning was tedious & dirty. Steel knives quickly became tarnished after being washed & they had to be polished. This process was performed on a knife board ~ where each blade was rubbed with a limestone block. The Victorian era saw the invention of the knife cleaning machine shown here. It could be fixed to a worktop or bolted to an iron stand.

CROSS SECTION
OF CLEANER
DISC · A =
LEATHER PADS.
B = LEATHER
BRUSHES.

KNIFE
BOARD

RUBBING STONE

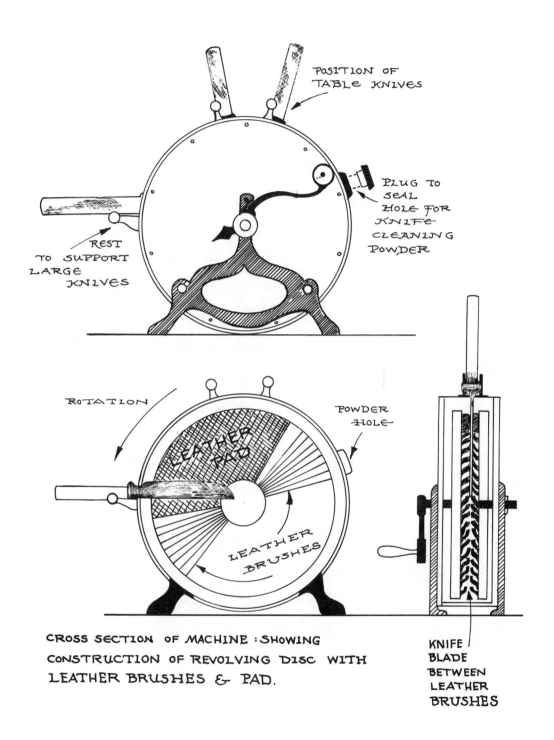

POSITION OF TABLE KNIVES

PLUG TO SEAL HOLE FOR KNIFE CLEANING POWDER

REST TO SUPPORT LARGE KNIVES

ROTATION

POWDER HOLE

LEATHER PAD

LEATHER BRUSHES

KNIFE BLADE BETWEEN LEATHER BRUSHES

CROSS SECTION OF MACHINE: SHOWING CONSTRUCTION OF REVOLVING DISC WITH LEATHER BRUSHES & PAD.

BUCKETS

The very refined buckets shown here were made
in mahogany & bound in brass. Some buckets
tell you their function by their distinctive
features: a PLATE PAIL had an open side that
allowed plates to be placed within or carefully
removed. Buckets, sometimes with a metal liner,
were also used for ice. The pineapple finial of
the WINE COOLER, with its pagoda top, was a
symbol of hospitality. Wine bottles were placed
on ice inside it. The tap was to draw off the
meltwater. The ubiquitous bucket shape ~ bottom
right ~ could be used for almost anything. Its
hipped sides would make it useful for logs or
winebottles. There is a similarity between the
wide & shallow OYSTER BUCKET, which stands
on its four-legged frame, & the KEELER used in
the dairy which allowed milk to settle so the
cream could be skimmed off.

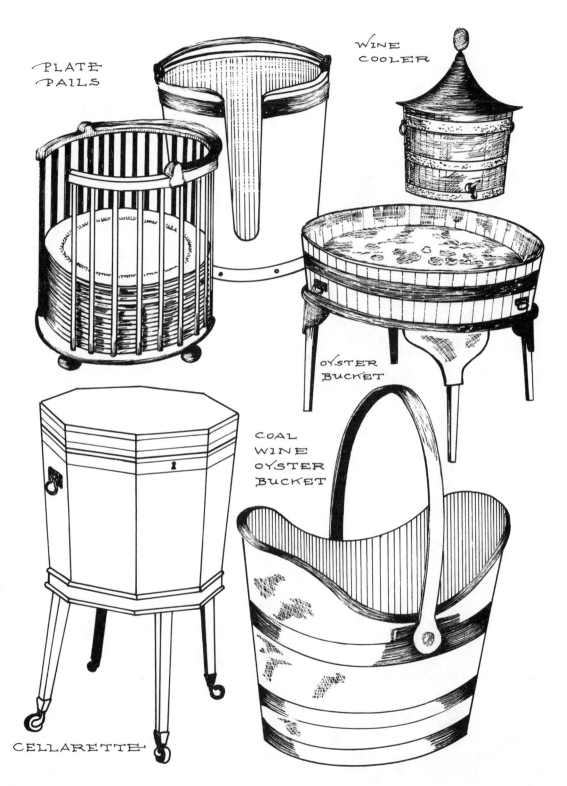

PLATE PAILS

WINE COOLER

OYSTER BUCKET

COAL
WINE
OYSTER
BUCKET

CELLARETTE

37

RUSHLIGHTS & CANDLES

Striking a light presented problems before
friction matches were invented ~c.1830.
Fire was created with a TINDER
BOX which had several parts.
The tinplate version
shown here has a
candleholder on its
outer lid ·1. The tinder·
2· was a piece of linen
which had to be kept very
dry. This was protected by
an inner lid·3· which kept
out damp air. To make a spark a
flint·4· was struck by a striker·5.
usually made from an old file. The sparks fell
onto the exposed linen & were blown upon until
it began to glow. This provided enough heat to
ignite a sulphur match·6. The flame was used
to light the candle. RUSHLIGHTS were
made from the pithy part of a peeled
rush. They were saturated in fat melted
in a gresset·A. In use the long, thin
rushlight was held in an iron stand
·B· which had jaws like a pair of
pliers.

TINDER BOX

Candles were too expensive to be used by all servants & some had to use rushlights. CANDLESTICK design slowly changed as new materials were introduced. The C17 examples ·8-9· were made in pewter or brass. By the C18 sticks ·10· had become heavier but still retained a drip tray ·x· to catch hot wax. Many Victorian candleholders were made of tinplate ·11· & were adjustable. A rustic form ·12· was also adjustable but it was a blacksmith's version with a wooden base. Within the house snuffers were used to extinguish candles as this lessened the smell.

Lanterns were used outside & in draughty passages ~ e.g. the hundred eyes example below.

CANDLE TAX
was abolished in 1837

Brass holder with glass chimney

Snuffer & Hundred eye Lantern.

OIL LAMPS

Oil was used for lighting even in prehistoric times. The method of burning oil was not efficient in primitive lamps like the crusie. A low level of light was obtained, & a lot of smoke. When spout lamps were used the same difficulties remained. From the mid~C18 until the 1860s much use was made of whale oil for lighting. Thousands of whales were sacrificed for this purpose. As the supply of whales declined vegetable oils were used. Colza oil, derived from oil seed rape, became popular. The greatest advance in light quality came when a glass chimney was added ~ the invention of Count Rumford. Flat & circular wicks, the latter devised by Aimé Argand c.1780, advanced the quality of light provided. Adjustable wicks changed the height & brightness of the flame.

WALL BRACKET LAMP WITH SOOT CATCHER

CRUSIE LAMP

OIL SOAKS UP THE WICK

SPOUT LAMP

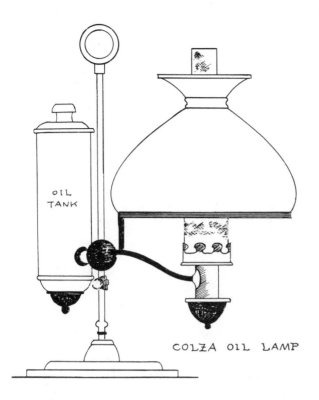

OIL
TANK

COLZA OIL LAMP

A

B

One disadvantage of vegetable oil was
its stickiness which caused the wicks to
need regular trimming. The introduction
of refined paraffin (1850) made a
great difference to domestic lighting.
If a lamp was always used in the
same position it could cause a sooty
patch to form on the ceiling above.

Many small lamps were produced
for carrying around the house ~
examples A + B were about eight
inches tall. The tiny night light~c~
had a weighted base so it could
not be tipped over.

C

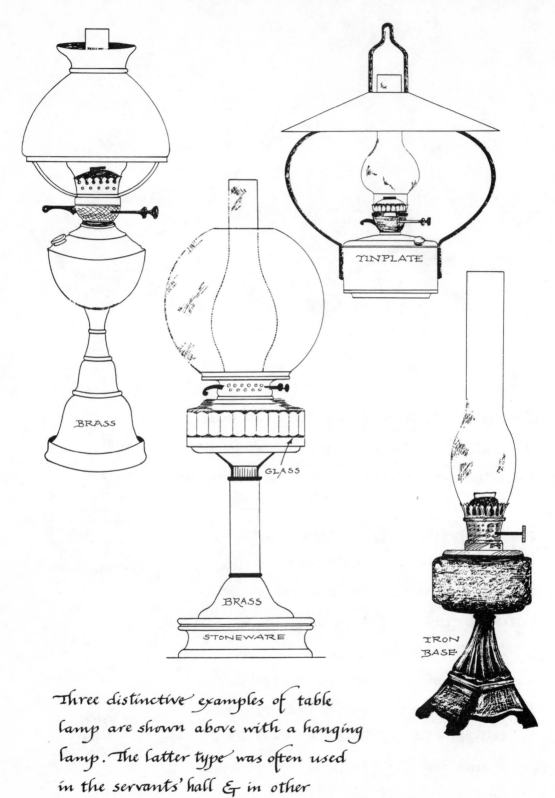

BRASS

GLASS

TINPLATE

BRASS

STONEWARE

IRON
BASE

Three distinctive examples of table
lamp are shown above with a hanging
lamp. The latter type was often used
in the servants' hall & in other
working places.

42

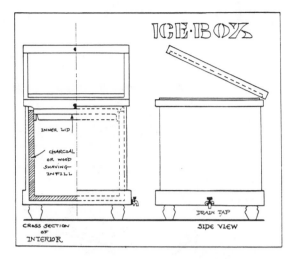

ICE·BOX

INNER LID

CHARCOAL OR WOOD SHAVING INFILL

DRAIN TAP

CROSS SECTION OF INTERIOR

SIDE VIEW

THE ICE BOX

Indoors ice boxes came into use during the C19, stocked with ice from an ICE HOUSE ~ see p. 126 . ICE BOXES were made of wood & had a double lining of zinc. Space between the inner lining was filled with an insulator ~ like wood shavings or charcoal. In chest-type boxes the food was surrounded by ice. It was not easy to get at the food placed at the bottom. Meltwater was removed via a draintap at the base. Like the Ice House an ice chest had an inner lid ~ in place of a second door ~ to reduce the rate of melting. In some places ice chests remained in daily use until the 1950s when domestic scale refridgerators became more widely available. Later C20 versions had an ice compartment placed at the top & a cupboard at the base. This type of ice box was an improvement on the chest and the contents were easier to remove.

43

THE LAUNDRY

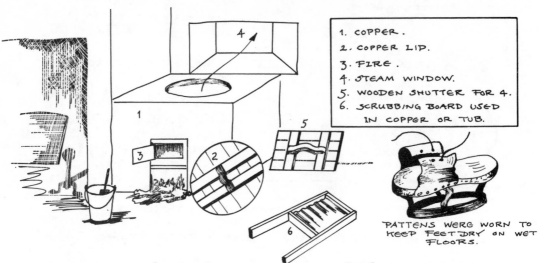

1. COPPER.
2. COPPER LIP.
3. FIRE.
4. STEAM WINDOW.
5. WOODEN SHUTTER FOR 4.
6. SCRUBBING BOARD USED
   IN COPPER OR TUB.

PATTENS WERG WORN TO
KEEP FEET DRY ON WET
FLOORS.

By C20 standards the equipment available was primitive & concentrated much on beating the dirt out by main force. Much of the washing was boiled in a 'copper', circular & round-bottomed filled with water & heated by a fire below. These were often built into the back kitchen near a fire. If possible the copper was placed near a window to allow the steam a ready exit. Cast-iron 'coppers' eventually replaced the brick versions.

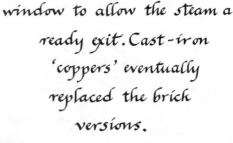

A · DOLLY FOR POUNDING WASHING
B · DOLLY TUB — GALVANISED
C · CAST IRON BOILER

44

IRONING

was always a tedious task
for the laundrymaids. As the
C19 progressed new forms of
iron appeared. The oldest type
of iron is the BOX IRON (A)
~ a legacy from C16 Holland ~
which was heated by placing a
red hot 'slug' inside. The solid, 'sad',
iron (B) was made in different weights.
CHARCOAL IRONS (C) were filled with
glowing charcoal ~ to keep them hot you
had to swing them to & fro.

A   BOX IRON

SLUG

SAD IRON

B

IRON
HOLDER

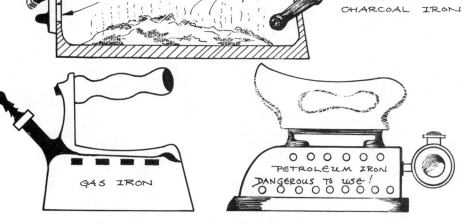

CATCH
TO
RELEASE
TOP

C

HAND GUARD

AIR VENT HOLE

MINIATURE
BELLOWS

USED ON A
CHARCOAL IRON

GAS IRON

PETROLEUM IRON
DANGEROUS TO USE!

45

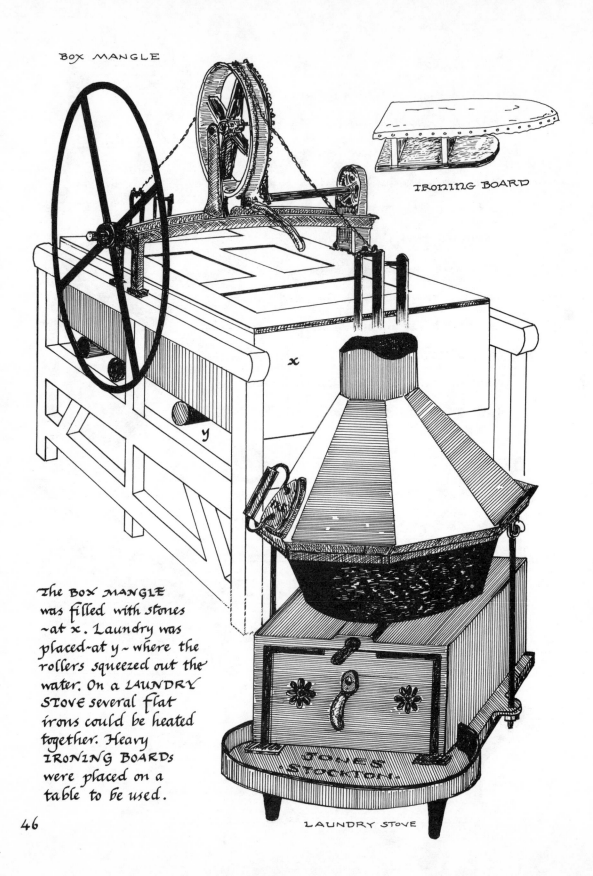

BOX MANGLE

IRONING BOARD

The BOX MANGLE was filled with stones ~at x. Laundry was placed~at y~ where the rollers squeezed out the water. On a LAUNDRY STOVE several flat irons could be heated together. Heavy IRONING BOARDS were placed on a table to be used.

LAUNDRY STOVE

Airing Rack

DRYING
RACKS
with
CENTRAL
STOVE ~
which also
heated irons.
Each rack
was moved
in & out
of the drying
areas on
the
rails set
in the floor.

As the C19 progressed technology
added to the range of laundry
aids. The first washing machines
appeared, but before electricity was
applied handpower was still essential.
When its legs were folded up this machine was rocked.

TRAPS

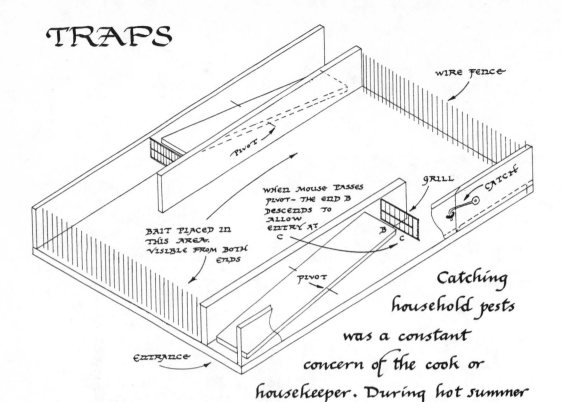

WIRE FENCE

PIVOT

WHEN MOUSE PASSES PIVOT – THE END B DESCENDS TO ALLOW ENTRY AT C

GRILL

CATCH

B C

BAIT PLACED IN THIS AREA. VISIBLE FROM BOTH ENDS

PIVOT

ENTRANCE

Catching household pests was a constant concern of the cook or housekeeper. During hot summer days flies were a great nuisance. The glass fly trap, opposite, captured flies by attracting them with a sugar solution ~ at x. The much messier sticky flypaper was once found in almost every house. It may have been effective but it was not an attractive item with its layer of insect bodies. MOUSETRAPS, before the invention of the spring trap, were home-made & probably the work of the estate carpenter. The double entry trap above had see-saw ramps which fell back after the mouse had passed by. We must guess at the fate of live mice captured. The DEADFALL traps ~ opposite ~ required the intruder to dislodge the carefully balanced levers ~ y & z ~ causing the weight to fall ~ with messy consequences.

48

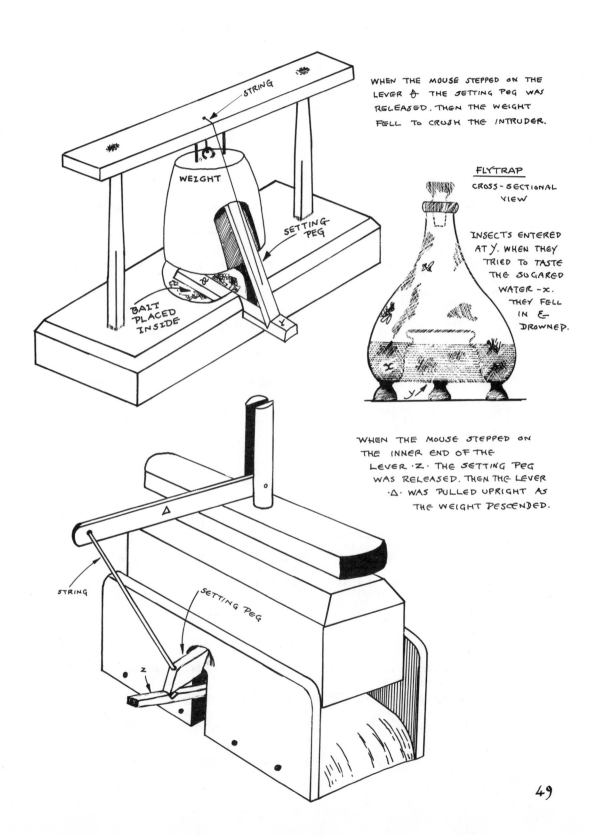

WHEN THE MOUSE STEPPED ON THE LEVER θ THE SETTING PEG WAS RELEASED. THEN THE WEIGHT FELL TO CRUSH THE INTRUDER.

STRING

WEIGHT

SETTING PEG

BAIT PLACED INSIDE

FLYTRAP
CROSS-SECTIONAL VIEW

INSECTS ENTERED AT y. WHEN THEY TRIED TO TASTE THE SUGARED WATER -x. THEY FELL IN & DROWNED.

WHEN THE MOUSE STEPPED ON THE INNER END OF THE LEVER ·Z· THE SETTING PEG WAS RELEASED. THEN THE LEVER ·Δ· WAS PULLED UPRIGHT AS THE WEIGHT DESCENDED.

STRING

SETTING PEG

49

WATER SUPPLY

If a Country House was placed below the level of a spring source, a piped supply fed by gravity was possible. Most houses, however, did not have a suitably placed spring. Their water had to be carried by hand, or provided by manual or animal powered pumps. If water was stored in a roof-level cistern even the upper floors could have a piped supply. It was commonplace in Victorian England to pump water to the top of a house by hand. On Sundays the servant who filled the storage tank received an additional shilling.

At ground level handpumps were very useful. These were made by the plumber & carpenter ~ see also Power Before Steam. These longcase pumps were to be found in kitchen courtyards; & some were indoors as a consequence of household extensions that gradually enclosed former open yards. The advantage of a pump was that it could be sited at some distance from the well.

One advantage of the cast iron pump which appeared in the latter part of the C19 was its size in relation to the longcase pump. These smaller alternatives were mass produced & they were widely used both indoors & out.

50

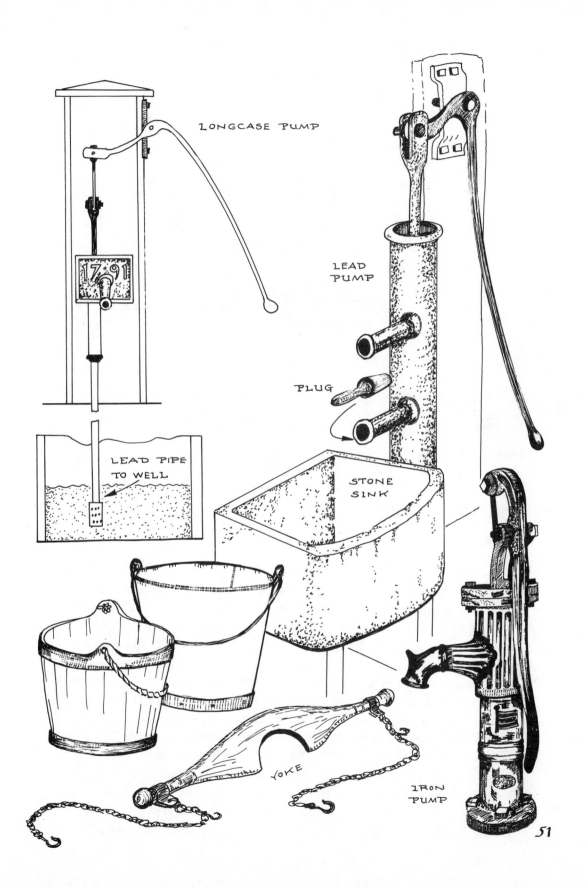

LONGCASE PUMP

17·91

LEAD PUMP

PLUG

LEAD PIPE
TO WELL

STONE
SINK

YOKE

IRON
PUMP

51

WATER RAM

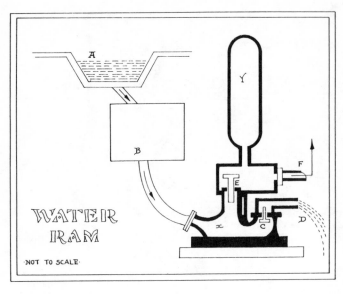

A

B

Y

F

E

WATER
RAM

x

C

D

·NOT TO SCALE·

Many readers will be familiar with the sudden thump in a water pipe if the supply is suddenly turned off. This percussive force is called 'water hammer.'

As long ago as 1797 Joseph Montgolfier, of the ballooning family, devised a model automatic pump which used this energy. It was not until the 1830s that the idea was applied, by a Mr. Easton in England, to a practical pump. His prototype was improved by John Blake of Accrington (in 1865) & his WATER RAM is still made today. The diagram shows how the RAM operates. Water from a stream A flows into a tank B. Then it flows, via the supply pipe, to the RAM. Within the chamber x the water reaches two valves~C & E. Before pressure builds up water can escape via C to the overflow at D. Increasing pressure closes valve C & then valve E is forced open. Water pushes into the air chamber Y & compresses the air. The pressure at x is reduced, valve C opens & water again runs to waste. As the pressure at Y is now greater valve E closes. The air at Y can then expand & push water up the pipe F. This cycle is repeated 50~200 times a minute depending upon water flow from B. A 4ft head of water can raise a supply some 300ft if the air chamber has a capacity of 6 cu.ft. A water ram can deliver 6000 galls. a day, & can work for years without trouble. It has two moving parts~valves C & E.

52 Many building were supplied with water in this way.

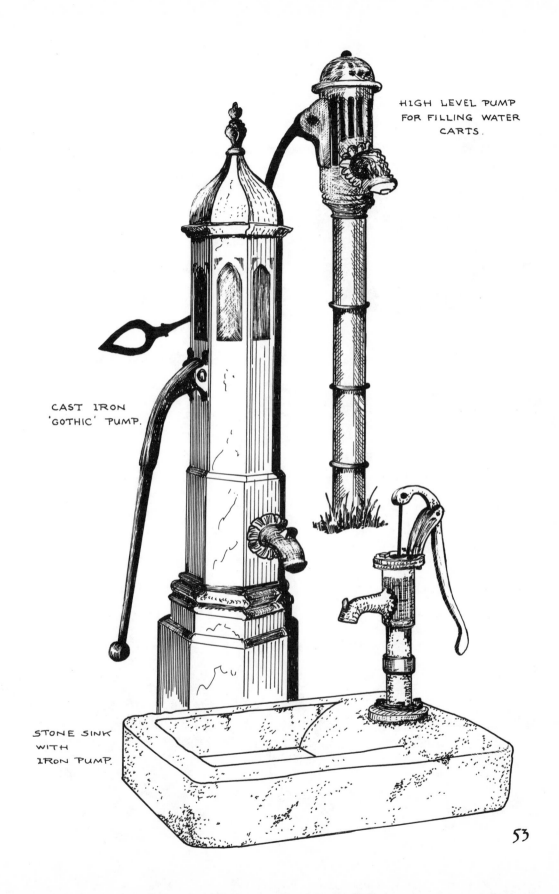

HIGH LEVEL PUMP
FOR FILLING WATER
CARTS.

CAST IRON
'GOTHIC' PUMP.

STONE SINK
WITH
IRON PUMP.

53

MUD SCRAPERS

The highways of Georgian England & the surroundings of country houses were, for a large part of every year, muddy. In the days before vacuum cleaners every housekeeper had to battle with dirt. We do not know who first devised the humble but effective mud scraper, but there is a strong possibility that the idea was contrived by a woman and fashioned by a blacksmith.

By the 1870s ironfounders were producing a wide variety of scraper designs. Some of these were set in a pan & could be carried away to be cleaned. The variation in features was reflected in the price ~ which could be one shilling & sixpence [7½p] or as much as nine shillings [45p]. Some mudscrapers were placed across a small recess close to a doorway.

WROUGHT IRON ACROSS A RECESS

54

TAXONOMY: There are several ways to attempt a classification of mud scrapers. This could be made by dividing them into wrought or cast-iron; or in terms of their style. It may be easier, however, to look at the number of fixing points. A few scrapers bear a maker's name but most are anonymous.

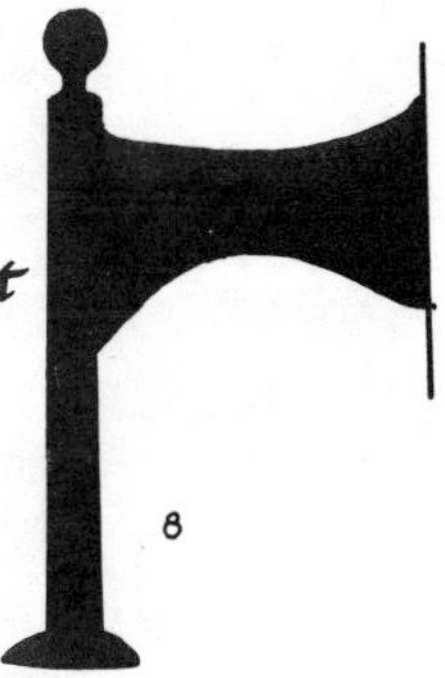

In the illustrations w = wrought iron & c = cast-iron :~:~:~:~:

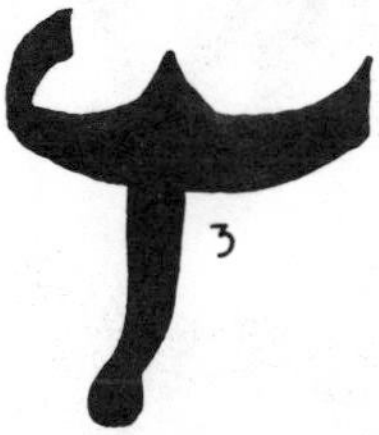

1w Stirrup · 2w Drop stirrup · 3w D-shaped · 4w D-shaped · 5w Single leg · 6c Single leg · 7w Single leg · 8w Single leg · 9w Single leg · 10w Stirrup · 11w Single leg · 12c Horse-shoe · 13c Bowl-shaped · 14, 15, 16w Stirrup type · 17w Two legs & buttresses · 18c Wall bracket · 19c Horse-shoe & finial · 20w Two legs & buttresses · 21w Two legs · 22c Spiked finials · 23c Button top · 24w Two long legs ~set by a step · 25c Vase-shaped · 26c Vase-shaped · 27c Gothic bridge · 28w Railing on steps · 29 & 30c Fireplace type · 31c Scissors pattern · 32w   Portable Georgian scraper~ the boot spade ·

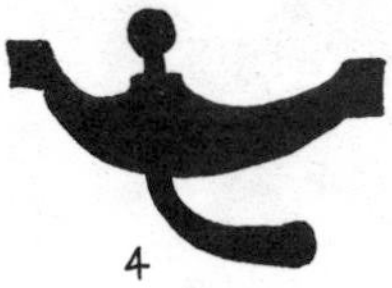

TALL LEG SET BY STEPS

ALWAYS LOOK FOR THE LEAD FILLING

LEAD PUDDLE

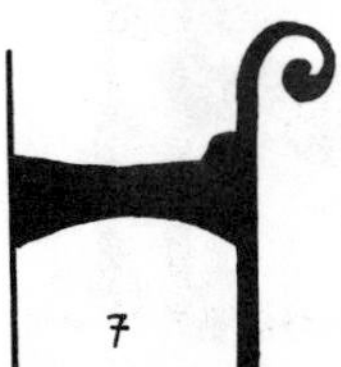

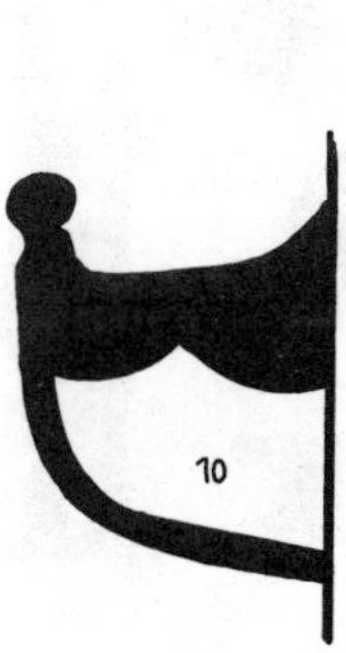

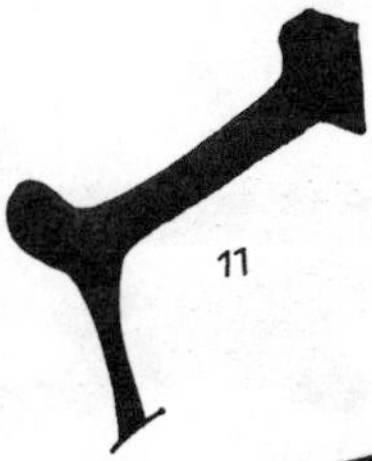

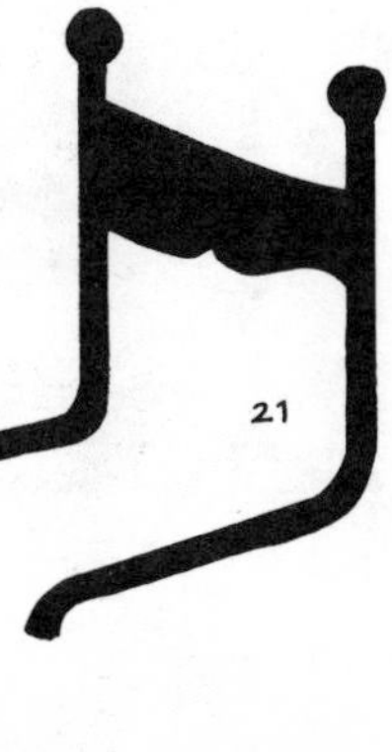

14

16

15

23

24

18

22

25

MUDSCRAPERS ARE
USUALLY ENCRUSTED &
DETAILS ARE NOT
EASY
TO
SEE

17

20

26

19

29

27

28

32

31

30

BOOTCLEANER

In addition to the mudscrapers above a mechanical device was produced to brush the mud off boots. This type of machine would have been used in a kitchen yard to allow gardeners or other visitors to clean their footwear before coming indoors. They were not elegant enough to be seen at an important entrance. Machines like this were probably made by a blacksmith. The author has not traced a manufacturer. To rotate the brush the handle was turned. The chain-drive, like a cycle's, is shown below.

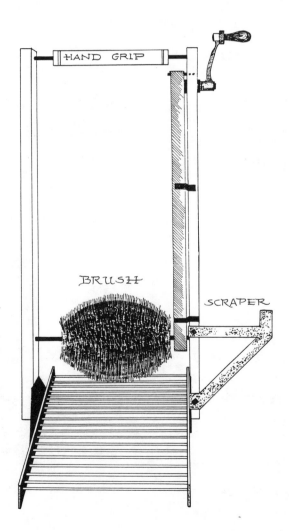

HAND GRIP

BRUSH

SCRAPER

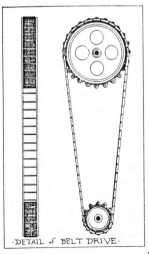

·DETAIL of BELT DRIVE·

57

THE HOUSE

THE HALL was a symbolic rather than a practical part of a household, a passing place ~ a link between the inner & private existence & the world without. It was a place to impress visitors & for that reason it had to be grand. Few people spent much time there, but seats were provided for lesser visitors who would expect to wait. This too was a place of vigil for the servant who had to wait up for members of the family who came home late. For such a purpose the hooded chair

HALL CHAIRS were not upholstered. Some displayed heraldic devices.

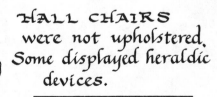

THIS EXAMPLE SHOWS VARIOUS GARDEN TOOLS ~ A SPADE, SPUDS for weeding, DIBBLERS. RAKES & HOES.

FIRE

IRON FIREPLACE

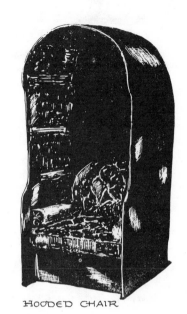

HOODED CHAIR

was provided to shelter the watcher from the cold night draughts. A hall usually had a fireplace, but it was seldom large enough to do more than imply warmth in so large a space.

FIREBUCKETS, an essential precaution before mains water came, were often close to the hall, but not always visible ~ being tucked away in a corridor. Old leather buckets often bore a family crest, or a monogram.

POST was taken by staff to the nearest post box & letters were left by the family in the hall. Household boxes, like the miniature pillar box shown here, were also used. The collection times are shown on the door~ plate. They remind us that households had established routines.

THE DINING ROOM

WINE WAS COOLED IN A METAL LINED DRAWER PARTLY FILLED WITH ICE

IN THE C18 NEW SOCIAL FASHIONS INVADED THE DINING ROOM

The old heavy oak & elm tables were replaced by more elegant alternatives in mahogany. Changes in the way dishes were served ~ by a footman presenting a given dish to a guest, instead of all the dishes being placed on the table at once ~ also affected the layout of the dining room. The butler presided over the sideboard & filled, refilled & washed the glasses. Water was obtained from an urn θ fitted with a tap. Dirty water could be discreetly disposed of in a bucket η concealed in a pedestal drawer. New artefacts appeared to add sophistication to the gentleman's table.

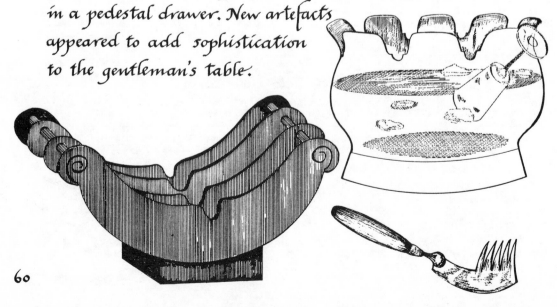

By the end of the Georgian era the idea of adjustable tables had been developed. This allowed the family to dine in close comfort when alone. For extra guests the table could quickly be enlarged. Furniture designers found different ways to fulfil this need, as these two tables show.

REGENCY
PERIOD·CENTRAL
PILLAR WITH CASTORS &
,HIDDEN, EXTRA LEAVES.
△ LEGS SWING OUT TO SUPPORT
ADDED LEAVES.

SLIDE

CIRCA 1820
PILLAR TABLE

EXTRA LEAF

The dining room had a masculine emphasis after the ladies had retired & Port was passed around. Hence the need for a wine table shown below.

OPPOSITE·····
LEFT·CHEESE COASTER.
RIGHT TOP·MONTEITH
~ devised to cool glasses in ice c.1683. It was named after its inventor. Made in silver & in porcelain. Monteiths were later used as Punch Bowls. BELOW. Combined knife & fork for use by a single hand. C18.

WINE TABLE
C. 1810

THE BOTTLE
HOLDERS OR
COASTERS MOVED
IN A SEMI-CIRCLE
AROUND SPINDLE
'A' WHICH WAS
FIXED TO RAIL 'B'.

61

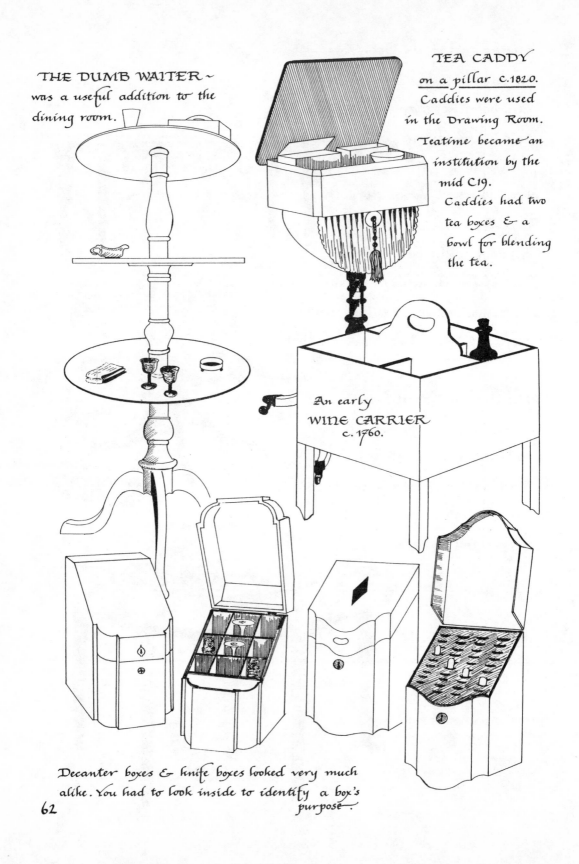

THE DUMB WAITER ~ was a useful addition to the dining room.

TEA CADDY on a pillar C.1820. Caddies were used in the Drawing Room. Teatime became an institution by the mid C19. Caddies had two tea boxes & a bowl for blending the tea.

An early WINE CARRIER c. 1760.

Decanter boxes & knife boxes looked very much alike. You had to look inside to identify a box's purpose.

62

THE LIBRARY

As the number of books increased in the C18 every country house had to have a library. Furniture designers began to produce pieces especially for them: tables or chairs which transformed into steps.

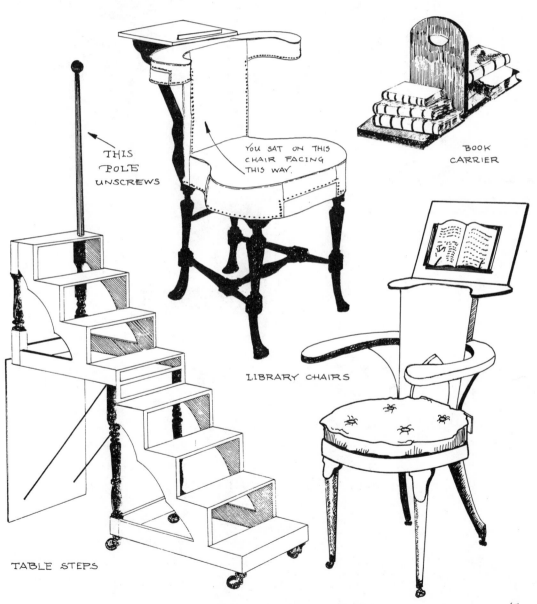

THIS POLE UNSCREWS

YOU SAT ON THIS CHAIR FACING THIS WAY.

BOOK CARRIER

LIBRARY CHAIRS

TABLE STEPS

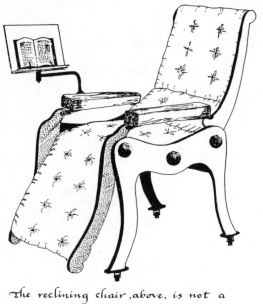

The reclining chair, above, is not a
modern invention. This one has
an adjustable leg rest & a
book rest.

Bookcases in the country
house were often very tall.
In addition to the library
steps which also served as
a table, designers
created
chairs which
could be converted
into steps. When closed
it was not always obvious
that a chair was a set of steps. The two examples
shown illustrate how they looked as a chair &
as steps. The seat pulled forward ✦ & the hinged
part then rested on the floor.

Fireside screens were important to ladies who did
not want the fire's heat to damage their complexions.
Screens were adjustable & often decorated with
needlepoint panels.

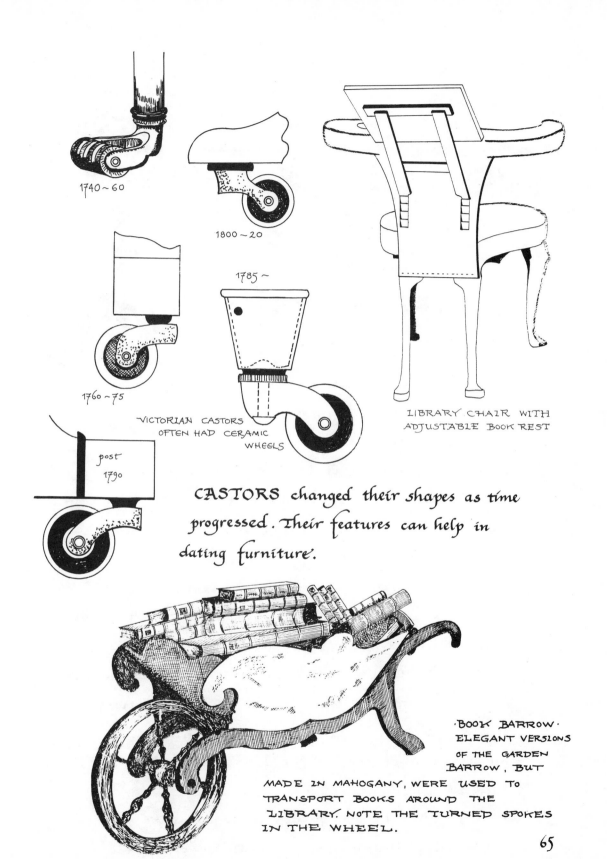

1740 ~ 60

1800 ~ 20

1785 ~

1760 ~ 75

VICTORIAN CASTORS
OFTEN HAD CERAMIC
WHEELS

LIBRARY CHAIR WITH
ADJUSTABLE BOOK REST

post
1790

CASTORS changed their shapes as time progressed. Their features can help in dating furniture.

·BOOK BARROW·
ELEGANT VERSIONS
OF THE GARDEN
BARROW, BUT
MADE IN MAHOGANY, WERE USED TO
TRANSPORT BOOKS AROUND THE
LIBRARY. NOTE THE TURNED SPOKES
IN THE WHEEL.

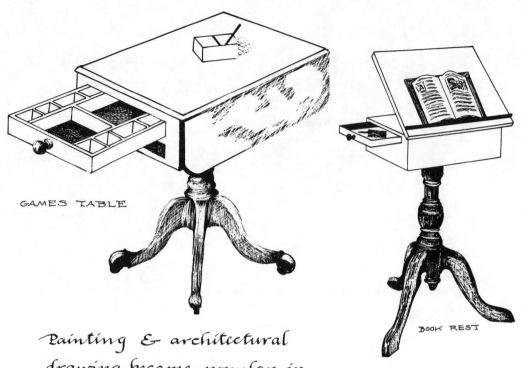

GAMES TABLE

BOOK REST

Painting & architectural
drawing became popular in
the C18. Designers began to
produce special artists' tables, now often described
as architects' tables in contemporary sale catalogues.
The candle slides were necessary & remind us of
the days before oil lamps.

The DRUM-TOP table, opposite, has a fold-down book
rest. This design is also known as a RENT-TABLE
if the drawers are alphabetically arranged = A-C,
D-F, G-J etc. On each quarter-day the owner, or
his agent, sat at the table to receive the rents from
tenant farmers & cottagers. Their individual pay-
ments were placed in the drawer appropriate to
their names.

On wet days the games table could be pushed
up to the library fire & used in comfort.

66

ARCHITECT'S TABLE

DRUMTOP TABLE

C19
MUSIC HOLDER —
A 'CANTERBURY'

67

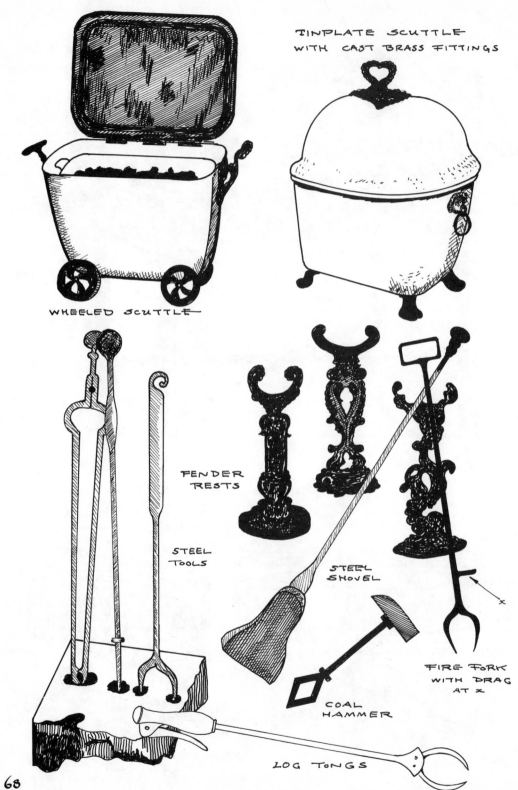

TINPLATE SCUTTLE
WITH CAST BRASS FITTINGS

WHEELED SCUTTLE

FENDER
RESTS

STEEL
TOOLS

STEEL
SHOVEL

FIRE FORK
WITH DRAG
AT X

x

COAL
HAMMER

LOG TONGS

68

FIRESIDE FURNITURE

HOUSEMAIDS spent many hours on their knees attending to the fires in the principal rooms of the house & in the bedrooms. Coal fires always produced a lot of dust and dirt. The coal supply was kept close to the fire in scuttles which were usually black but still showed the dust. Some scuttles had wheels. Those shown here have inner linings that could be lifted out. Fenders were heavy and elaborate. There were bright steel or brass parts to some & these had to be kept polished. Tools like the tongs & poker were often made in brass. Cast-iron rests were used to support them. Additional tools like log tongs also became popular. Some hand bellows were elaborately decorated.

ABOVE · CHIMNEY BOARD · THESE WERE DECORATED BOARDS PLACED IN THE FIREPLACE DURING SUMMER TO HIDE THE EMPTY GRATE & CATCH ANY SOOT. THEY OFTEN DISPLAYED CLASSICAL OR HERALDIC DESIGNS.

BELLOWS

THE HOUSEMAID'S BOX contained all the necessary equipment for work about the fire. This heavy load was carried from room to room with its collection of brushes, abrasives, cleaning rags & polishes. Each morning the ashes were taken from every fireplace and placed in the ash box. This limited the amount of dust discharged into the room but did not eliminate it. The curved base of the ash box allowed it to be rocked causing the ash to fall to the bottom.

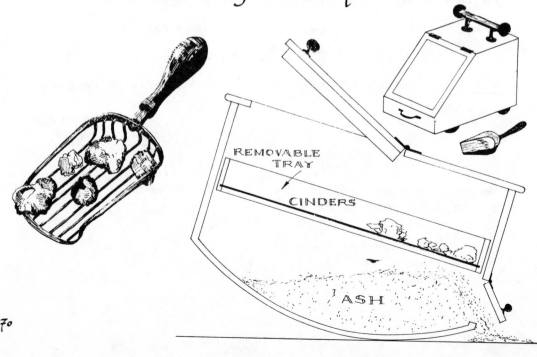

REMOVABLE TRAY

CINDERS

ASH

THE BEDROOM

The Georgians' beds were still modelled on the protected four posters of the past with their draught-excluding curtains. The C18 versions had very rich drapery indeed ~ like the splendid example at Calke Abbey. An additional purpose of these draperies, in mediaeval times, was to save the occupants from bird

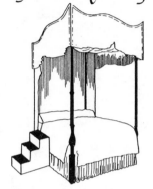

droppings. The Georgians had made their houses birdproof. Eaves were closed and windows glazed.

Most bedrooms in the C18 had fireplaces. Keeping warm was always a problem in winter, & damp beds could be avoided by using a warming pan [p.72] filled with hot coals or charcoal.

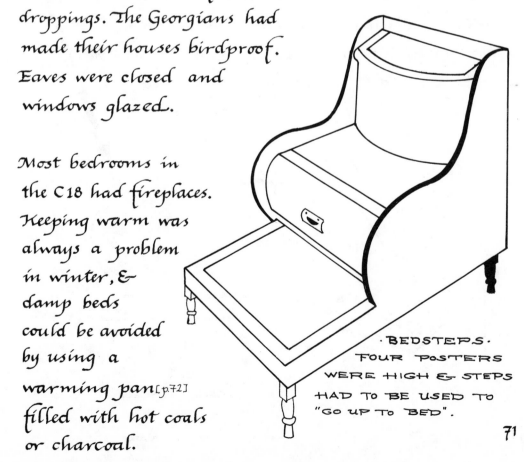

· BEDSTEPS ·
FOUR POSTERS WERE HIGH & STEPS HAD TO BE USED TO "GO UP TO BED".

The warm pan was moved around the bed to warm the sheets – hence the long handle.

After use the coals had to be removed so that the pan could be hung on its wall hook.

Bedside cabinets came into use in the C18. They often had a dual purpose like the one shown above, which has a sliding section containing a chamber pot. A lesser alternative was the close stool with a removable or hinged lid. The seat was upholstered for extra comfort.

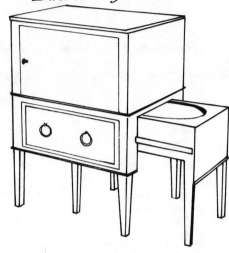

BEDSIDE CABINET.
WITH SLIDING STOOL.
EARLY C19.

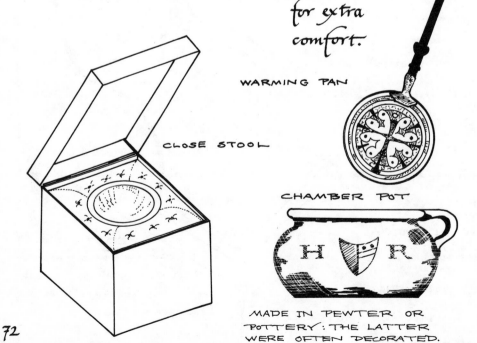

WARMING PAN

CLOSE STOOL

CHAMBER POT

MADE IN PEWTER OR POTTERY: THE LATTER WERE OFTEN DECORATED.

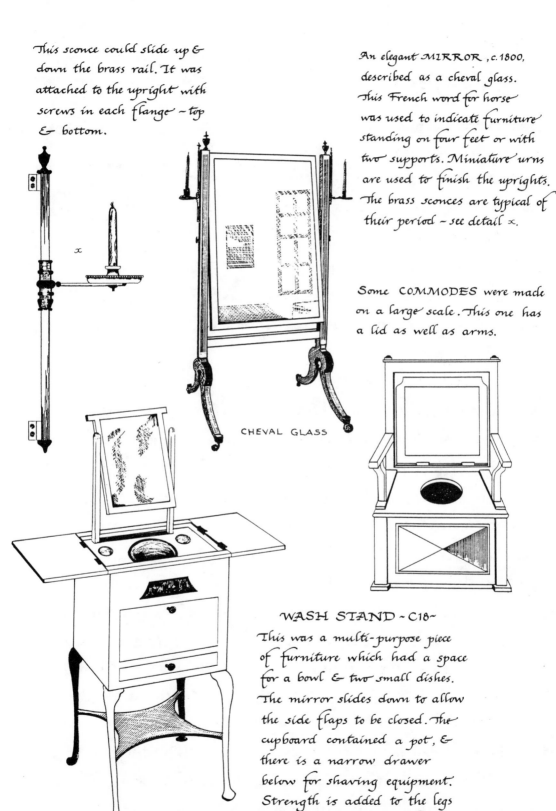

This sconce could slide up & down the brass rail. It was attached to the upright with screws in each flange — top & bottom.

x

An elegant MIRROR, c.1800, described as a cheval glass. This French word for horse was used to indicate furniture standing on four feet or with two supports. Miniature urns are used to finish the uprights. The brass sconces are typical of their period — see detail x.

Some COMMODES were made on a large scale. This one has a lid as well as arms.

CHEVAL GLASS

WASH STAND ~ C18~

This was a multi-purpose piece of furniture which had a space for a bowl & two small dishes. The mirror slides down to allow the side flaps to be closed. The cupboard contained a pot, & there is a narrow drawer below for shaving equipment. Strength is added to the legs with the delicate shelf.

73

THE BATHROOM

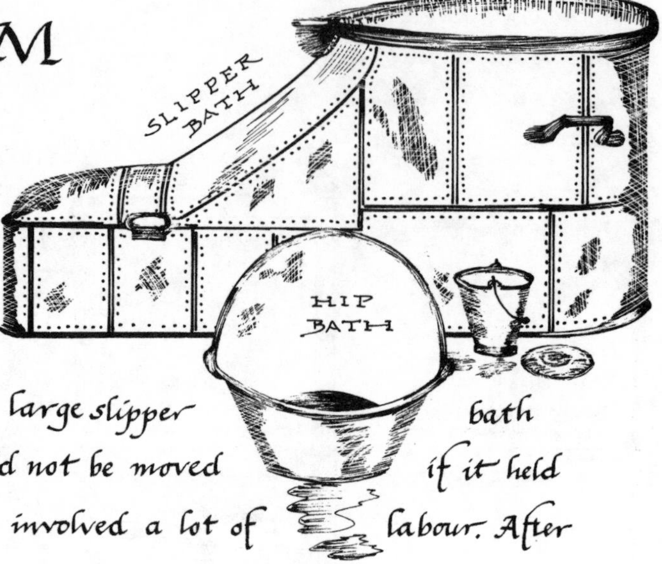

Large amounts of hot water were needed for baths & before a piped supply was available it all had to be carried by the housemaids. This large slipper has four handles. It could not be moved water. Even a hip bath involved a lot of bath if it held labour. After use all the water had to be carried away.

SLIPPER BATH

HIP BATH

Technology came to the rescue of the housemaids. Once a storage tank had been provided at roof level it was possible to supply water upstairs. A piped source and a fixed bath allowed a boiler to be added. This was the same type of boiler used in a laundry, & its contents were heated by a coal fire. Fuel, of course, still had to be carried upstairs by the housemaids. The system shown opposite works in the following way ~

A cold water supply is piped from A ←. There is a tap B which can provide cold water directly into the bath. At the end of the pipe a second tap C delivers water to the boiler D. When heated the hot water could be supplied to the bath by using the tap E. Notice how the boiler is raised on a brick plinth to allow the water to fall to the lower level of the bath F. There is an overflow G which discharges into the pipe → J.

74

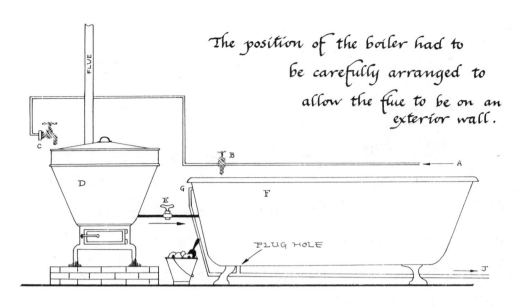

The position of the boiler had to be carefully arranged to allow the flue to be on an exterior wall.

PLUG HOLE

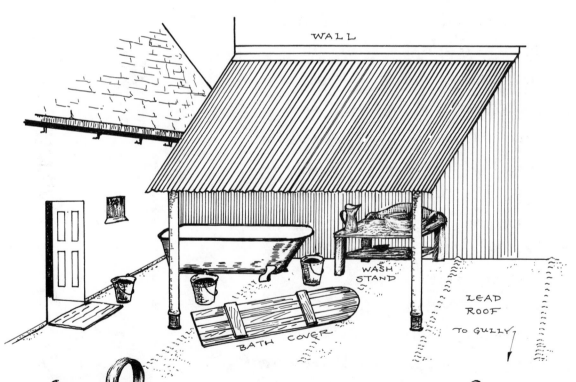

WALL

WASH STAND

LEAD ROOF

TO GULLY

BATH COVER

WATER CARRIER

COLD BATHS were a part of the Victorian culture. This example is placed outdoors on a roof with a lean-to shelter to protect the user from the rain.

75

WATER CLOSET

POT CUPBOARD
· WITH RECEPTACLE ··

THE POLITE Georgian country house had a POT CUPBOARD hidden away behind the folding shutters of the dining room ~ for gentlemen to use after the ladies had retired from dinner, and much port had been drunk. The idea of the water closet dates from the 17th. century but little use was made of it until the 19th. century. We should not forget, however, that even in the 1950s earth closets were still to be found serving some estate cottages! The heights of plumbing excellence were reached, post 1851, when the automatic cistern was introduced.

Engineers contrived cast-iron tanks, ceramic pedestals & mahogany seats. The water supply was derived from tanks in the attic, which were sometimes filled by rainwater.

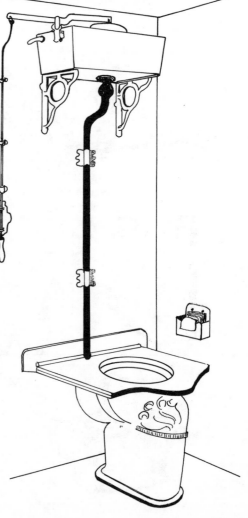

KEEPING FIT

The great appetites of the C18, whetted by new ingredients, were matched by a new emphasis upon health & thousands of gentry made their way to the important spa towns – like Bath & Buxton. These became important social centres, & second homes for thousands of families who took part in the annual migrations. One condition which attracted sufferers to the spas was gout – an hereditary & painful swelling of the joints which affected males. A specific item of furniture made for the gout sufferer was the GOUT STOOL. This tripod stool could be adjusted to the required height & inclination. It represents the way in which craftsmen responded to new needs, often combining wood & metal. The C18 saw the engineer beginning to contribute to the cabinet maker's designs.

CHAMBER HORSE · SEE p.78.

A curious addition to the catalogue of furnishings developed in the Georgian period was the special chair used for exercising ~ i.e. jumping up and down in a sedentary position.

Whatever the value of such exercise the design of these CHAMBER HORSES provided new challenges for the furniture makers. Most chamber horses have a step at the front, and arms for the sitter to grip.

The deep cushion hides the several layers of springs (b) which are supported on dividing boards (c). As the sitter bounced up and down air was expelled via the air holes (a). For extra comfort the seat top (d) had additional padding.

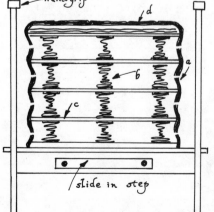

hand grip

d

a

b

c

slide in step

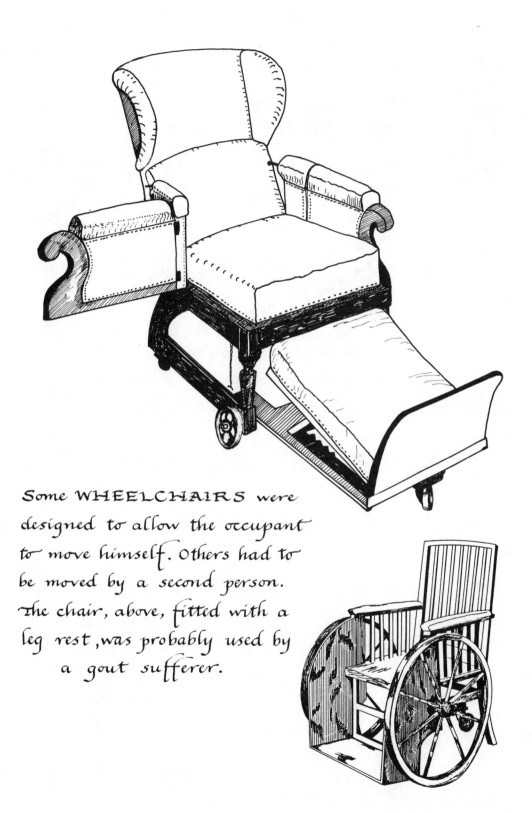

Some WHEELCHAIRS were
designed to allow the occupant
to move himself. Others had to
be moved by a second person.
The chair, above, fitted with a
leg rest, was probably used by
a gout sufferer.

THE ESTATE

In many ways the business of estate management was more complex than that of the household. There were more elements to be overseen by the ESTATE MANAGER or AGENT who was answerable to the MASTER. The illustration above, from a mural on an estate cottage, reminds us how the workers viewed those who ordered their lives.

The diagram opposite shows the various aspects of the working estate. There was little overlap between the estate & house staff, but the gardener provided the cook with fruit & vegetables & was a daily visitor to the kitchen. The grooms too had regular contact with household affairs as they provided transport.

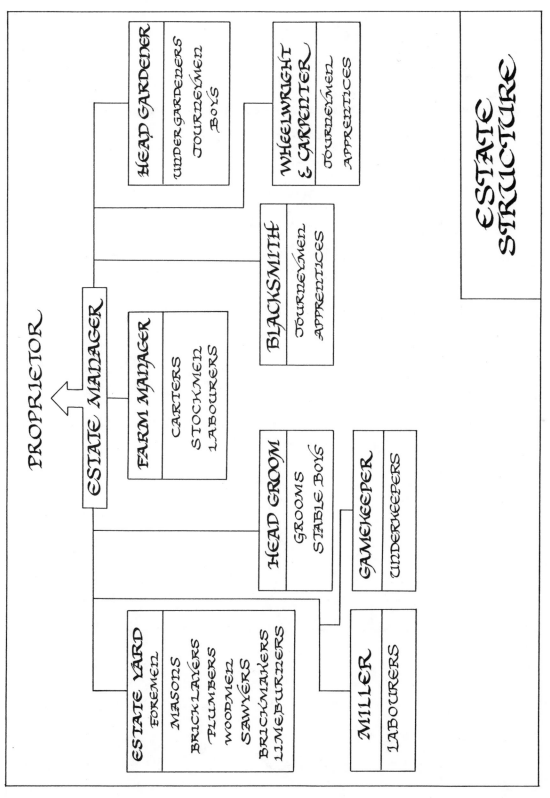

ESTATE STRUCTURE

PROPRIETOR

ESTATE MANAGER

HEAD GARDENER
UNDERGARDENERS
JOURNEYMEN
BOYS

WHEELWRIGHT & CARPENTER
JOURNEYMEN
APPRENTICES

BLACKSMITH
JOURNEYMEN
APPRENTICES

FARM MANAGER
CARTERS
STOCKMEN
LABOURERS

HEAD GROOM
GROOMS
STABLE BOYS

GAMEKEEPER
UNDERKEEPERS

ESTATE YARD
FOREMEN
MASONS
BRICKLAYERS
PLUMBERS
WOODMEN
SAWYERS
BRICKMAKERS
LIMEBURNERS

MILLER
LABOURERS

THE GARDEN

The C18 landowner began to enjoy the longer prospects from his own windows. CAPABILITY BROWN developed the fashion for landscape gardens, a total contrast to the enclosed formal and symmetrical gardens of the C17. These new landscapes were enhanced with clumps & belts of trees and elaborate garden buildings ~ temples & prospect towers. The parkland had to provide grazing for deer and cattle, but it was necessary to keep livestock away from the gardens close to the house itself. Fences could detract from the prospect but by constructing a HA HA the scenery could be enjoyed without a visual barrier. The term HA HA derives from the surprise of finding an unexpeted precipice.

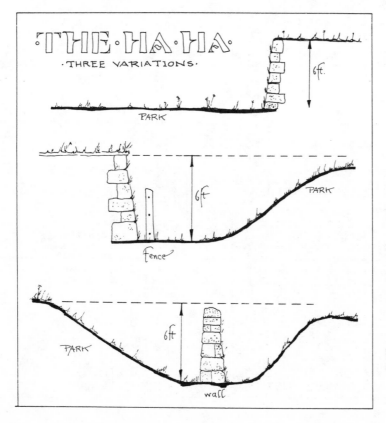

THE·HA·HA·
·THREE VARIATIONS·

PARK
6ft.

6ft
PARK
fence

PARK
6ft
wall

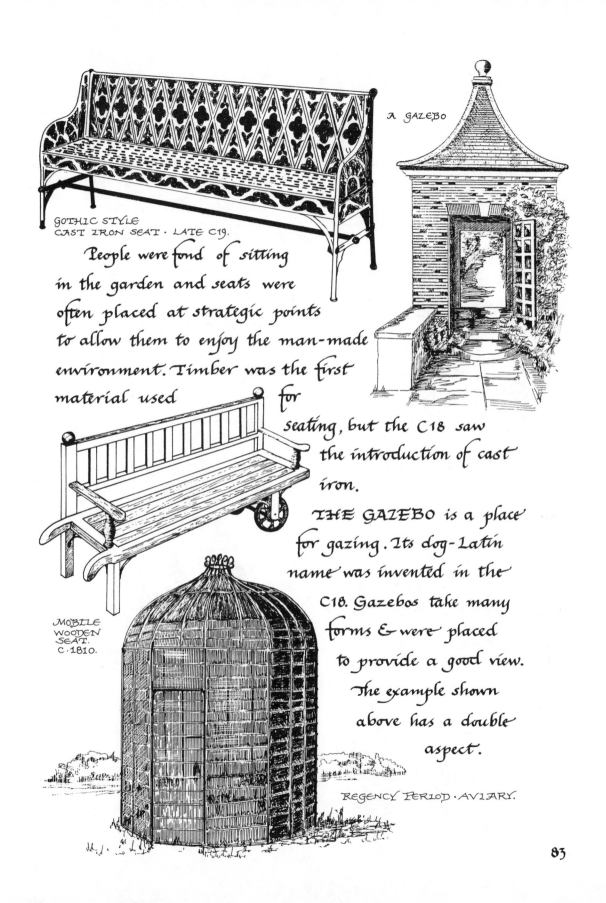

GOTHIC STYLE
CAST IRON SEAT · LATE C19.

A GAZEBO

People were fond of sitting in the garden and seats were often placed at strategic points to allow them to enjoy the man-made environment. Timber was the first material used for seating, but the C18 saw the introduction of cast iron.

THE GAZEBO is a place for gazing. Its dog-Latin name was invented in the C18. Gazebos take many forms & were placed to provide a good view. The example shown above has a double aspect.

MOBILE
WOODEN
SEAT.
C·1810.

REGENCY PERIOD · AVIARY.

83

FOLLIES & EYECATCHERS

One feature of the C18 estate was the fashion for creating eyecatching landmarks. These idiosyncratic buildings often formed part of a large landscape gardening scheme. They were the punctuation marks, as it were, of the views & vistas.

The very tall buildings like Broadway Tower, Glos. (1797), gave commanding views of the surrounding country.

Right: The Needle's Eye, Wentworth Woodhouse, Yorks. (1780)
Below: Rousham Eyecatcher, Oxon. (c. 1740).

~TOPIARY~

The art of making green sculptures in the garden probably dates from the Roman period. Box was commonly used for topiary forms, but juniper, privet, whitethorn, & latterly yew were also grown. Gardeners used special clippers to make & maintain these special shapes.

LAWN MOWING

In the C18 the grass of great houses was kept short by grazing animals & by scythes. The close cropped lawn became fashionable after the invention of the first mower ~ by Edwin Budding, 1830. He developed his mower from a machine used for removing the pile on cloth. Another forty years passed before a horse-drawn mower was introduced ~ 1870 ~ though they had been used in agriculture since 1800. Horses can easily leave a hoof print on a soft surface so they were provided with 'slippers'. One type of slipper was secured with a set screw, but the strap-on kind were more common. Eventually steam power invaded the nation's lawns in 1893.

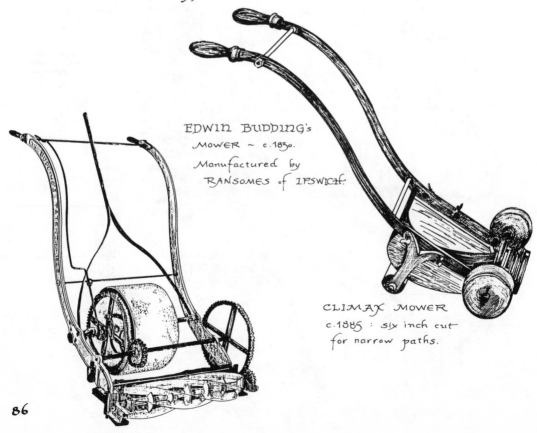

EDWIN BUDDING's
MOWER ~ c.1830.
Manufactured by
RANSOMES of IPSWICH.

CLIMAX MOWER
c.1885 : six inch cut
for narrow paths.

When a lawn was damaged it could be repaired by using a turf spade. This tool could remove the damaged area after it had been cut around by a common spade. An edging tool, used in conjunction with a line, helped to keep a tidy appearance. The condition of the lawn was maintained by using a pricker. Early mowers left the cut grass to be collected by hand. This was a job for a garden boy armed with a rake, broom & barrow.

A ~ Stone roller
B ~ Wooden roller
C ~ Line
D ~ Turf spade
F ~ Lawn pricker
G ~ Lawn broom
H ~ Horse slipper

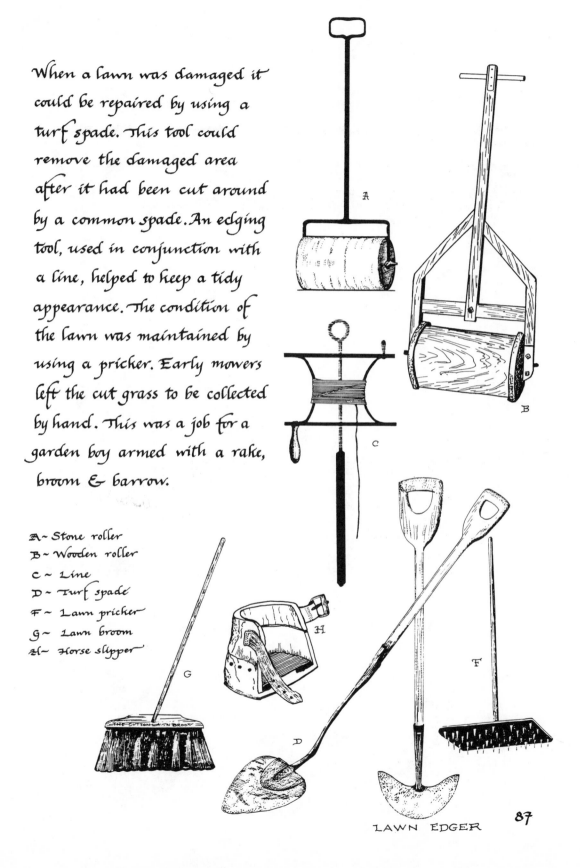

LAWN EDGER

87

LAWN GAMES

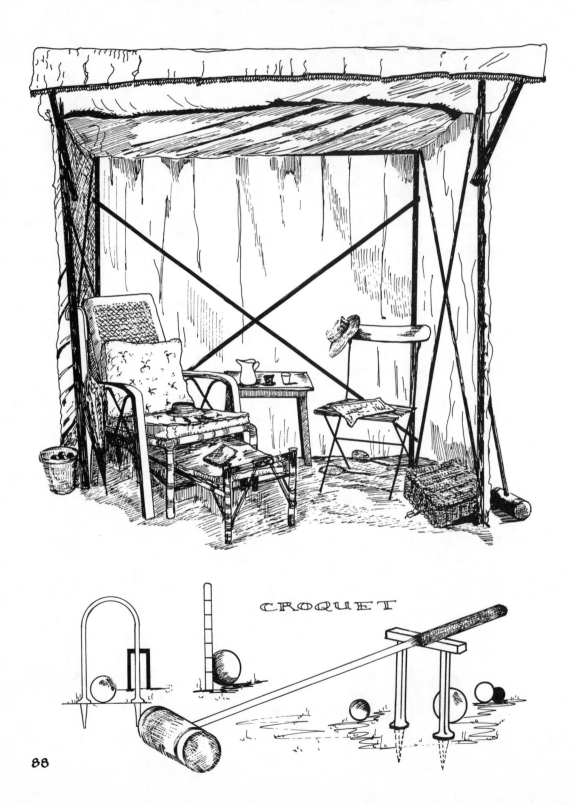

CROQUET

ONCE it became possible to provide & maintain a lawn, many genteel games were developed to make use of the green space. Croquet, archery, lawn golf ~ putting, tennis & cricket all found a place in this new repertoire. Some objects, like the cricket barrow, were probably one-off creations made to meet specific needs. For the less energetic canvas awnings were made to provide shade & shelter for chairs & tables.

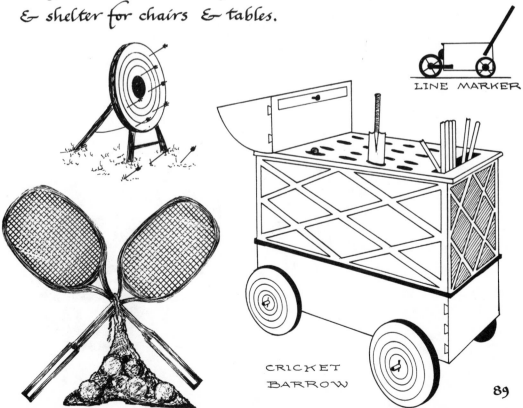

LINE MARKER

CRICKET BARROW

89

BARROWS

BARROWS appear in C17 books on horticulture, but the genius who first thought of the idea remains anonymous. There are two kinds of barrow. One was designed to carry a loose load and its capacity could be increased by the addition of sideboards ~ the same method was used to add to the farmer's tip cart. A removable back board, which fitted into slots, was a feature of some barrows. This allowed the contents to be taken out with a shovel. Barrows were built by the wheelwright ~ carpenter. As the C19 progressed the common barrow was manufactured in the factory. The cost of a barrow ~ c.1918 ~ was about £3. Sideboards were an extra 25 shillings.

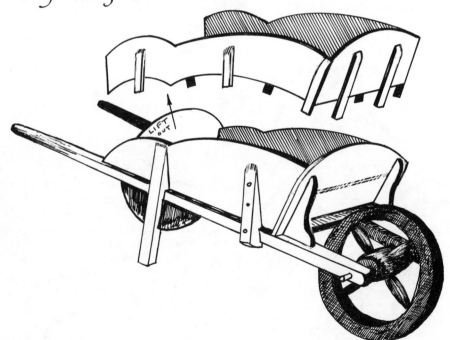

FLATBARROWS were used to carry boxes of seeds or plants as well as tools. Work in the garden required constant movement of materials & tools. A busy garden needed several barrows. GARDENING became a popular activity for ladies & gentlemen during Victoria's reign. We do not know exactly what the professional gardeners thought of this intrusion into their working lives. Manufacturers however were quick to provide suitable 'genteel' equipment for those who wished to engage in gardening. The quality & finish of a lady's mahogany barrow provides its own commentary.

PRUNING & CUTTING

Various tools were devised to perform these necessary tasks - which required sawing, chopping, clipping or cutting. The tools shown here are: A~ A Grecian saw which cost three shillings in 1906. B~ Pruning hooks for gooseberries had long handles to help the user avoid the prickles. C~ The gardener's knife. D~ Asparagus knife. E~ Vine secateurs with axe blade. F~ Sliding action pruner. G~ Folding saw, cutting on the pulling stroke. H~ Slashers. I~ Tree pruner with 3 cutting edges. J~ Grass hook, also used in harvest work. K~ Bill hook, a tool with many alternative shapes. Kk~ Whetstone used for sharpening edged tools. L~ Combined saw & hook. M~ Pruning saw with a blade that folded into the stick.[A dual purpose but not very practical tool.] N~ This multi-purpose tool was a walking stick, saw & weeding spud. O & P~ Pruning saws, one with a double edge. Q~ The ever useful hand axe.

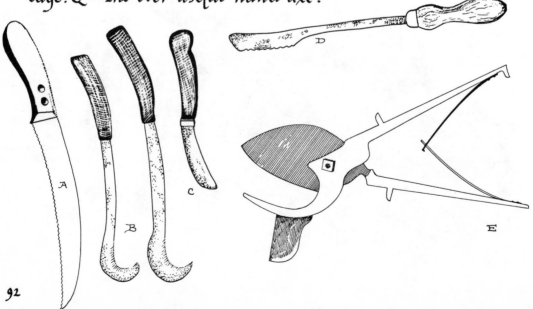

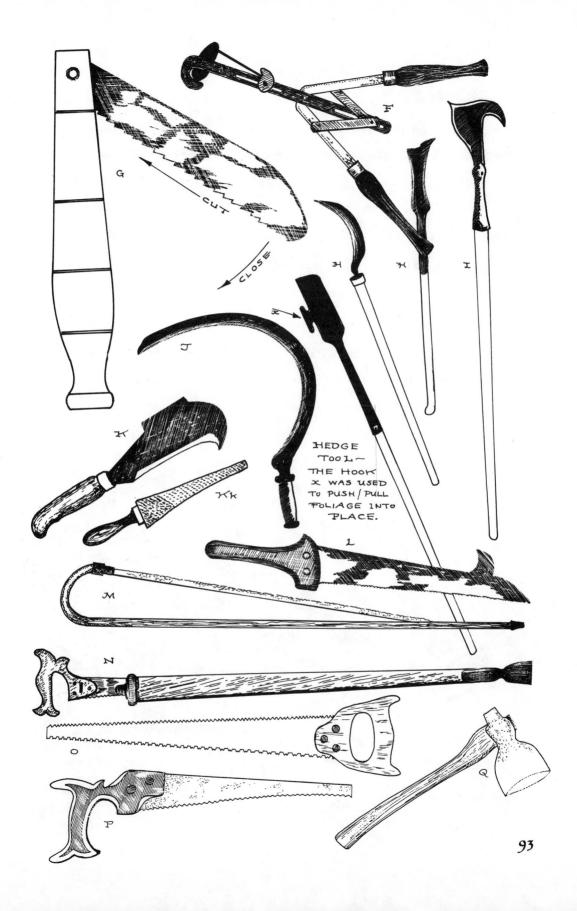

G

CUT

CLOSE

F

H

K

I

J

K

Kk

HEDGE
TOOL —
THE HOOK
X WAS USED
TO PUSH / PULL
FOLIAGE INTO
PLACE.

L

M

N

O

P

Q

93

THE GREENHOUSE

A great deal of time was spent in the greenhouse which played an important part in the household economy. The skill of the gardener provided fresh fruit & vegetables throughout the winter months. The produce of the garden & greenhouse was not used in the great house alone. Many families had a second home in London, or perhaps another significant town like Bath, to which produce would be regularly sent in large wicker baskets by road or rail. Not all employers trusted their staff, especially in the hard days of the 1880s, when agriculture was in decline. The notice shown here may tell us more about the employer than the workmen.

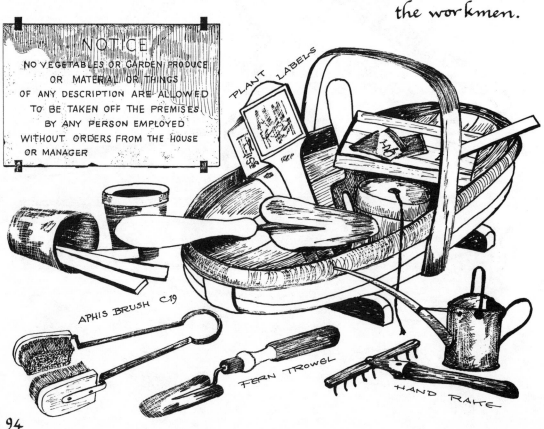

NOTICE

NO VEGETABLES OR GARDEN PRODUCE OR MATERIAL OR THINGS OF ANY DESCRIPTION ARE ALLOWED TO BE TAKEN OFF THE PREMISES BY ANY PERSON EMPLOYED WITHOUT ORDERS FROM THE HOUSE OR MANAGER

PLANT LABELS

APHIS BRUSH C19

FERN TROWEL

HAND RAKE

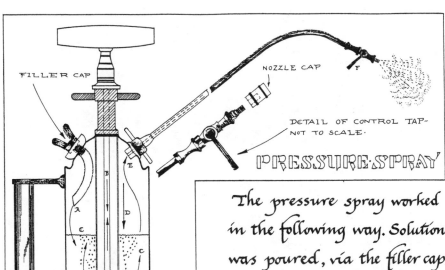

FILLER CAP

NOZZLE CAP

DETAIL OF CONTROL TAP-
NOT TO SCALE.

PRESSURE·SPRAY

The pressure spray worked in the following way. Solution was poured, via the filler cap, into the cylinder (A). Then the pump (B) was operated. This worked in the manner of a cycle pump with a plunger & leather washer (x). Air was expelled (y) & filled the space (c) in the upper cylinder. As the air pressure increased (D) it became powerful enough to expel the solution, via (E), when the control tap (F) was opened. Then the internal energy was released. The resulting spray was used to dress foliage in the greenhouse or garden.

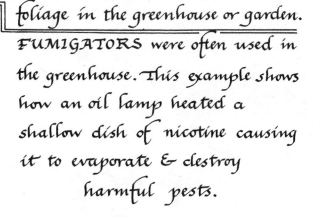

NICOTINE VAPOUR

OIL LAMP

FUMIGATORS were often used in the greenhouse. This example shows how an oil lamp heated a shallow dish of nicotine causing it to evaporate & destroy harmful pests.

95

PLANTING

SEED SIEVE

BIRD SCARER

A great deal depended upon the skills of those who worked in the POTTING SHED. A bird scarer η hangs from the shelf & a pot brush ϑ is shown below the bench.

Watering was a regular task. Watering cans came in several sizes and some had long spouts to reach awkward areas. Victorian cans were galvanised, but the first watering cans were made of clay. A rose was an important part of a can breaking up the flow & preventing seedlings from

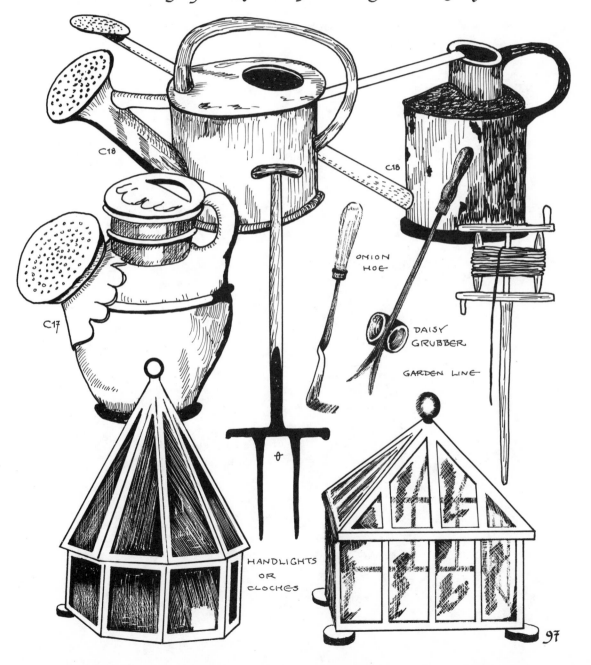

C18

C18

C17

ONION HOE

DAISY GRUBBER

GARDEN LINE

HANDLIGHTS
OR
CLOCHES

being washed away. Cloches of cast-iron were made in various shapes. A ring at the apex helped when they had to be moved. Clay forcing pots were common items. Some have survived the ravages of time. They were used for Sea Kale & Rhubarb. Weeding tools made from broken tools were used-like the fork ⊕. Hand weeding tools have distinctive shapes to improve leverage.

BELL CLOCHES

PLANT LABEL

BIRD SCARER

FORCING POTS

SPUD

RAINWATER

Rainwater was collected from the roof & stored in tanks for use in the garden. Guttering was first made of wood but by the C17 lead had replaced this basic material. Water discharged into a rainwater head & via downpipes into cisterns. Initials, dates, crests & shields of arms can often be found on lead furniture. It is quite likely that some lead-work you may encounter is not in its original position. When more durable cast-iron was introduced leadwork was often relocated on outbuildings.

THE STABLES

HORSEPOWER was important & sometimes stable blocks are more distinguished buildings than the houses they served. They were always close to and often incorporated a coach house. Grooms worked long hours & had to be able to prepare a conveyance at any time of day or night. As the use of cast iron was developed old stable fittings were replaced by this new material. It was durable & easy to keep clean. In the example shown below there are two stalls & two loose boxes. Each compartment has a manger & hay rack. Iron was also used for the stable gutters. Stable staff dealt with ailments & were responsible for the horses' appearance. Some of their everyday tools are shown opposite.

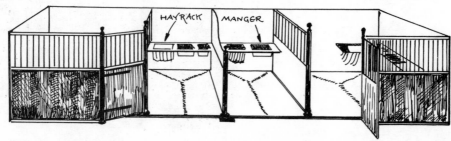

HAYRACK MANGER

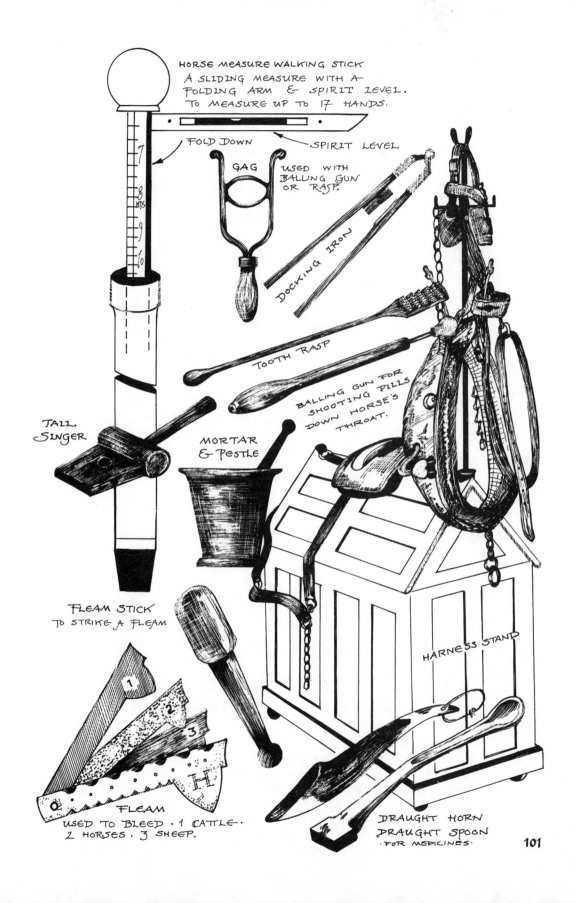

HORSE MEASURE WALKING STICK
A SLIDING MEASURE WITH A
FOLDING ARM & SPIRIT LEVEL.
TO MEASURE UP TO 17 HANDS.

FOLD DOWN   SPIRIT LEVEL

GAG   USED WITH
BALLING GUN
OR RASP.

DOCKING IRON

TOOTH RASP

BALLING GUN FOR
SHOOTING PILLS
DOWN HORSE'S
THROAT.

TAIL
SINGER

MORTAR
& PESTLE

FLEAM STICK
TO STRIKE A FLEAM

HARNESS STAND

FLEAM
USED TO BLEED · 1 CATTLE ·
2 HORSES · 3 SHEEP.

DRAUGHT HORN
DRAUGHT SPOON
· FOR MEDICINES ·

101

WEATHERVANES

THE WEATHER has always been a preoccupation of the English. Knowing which way the wind was blowing became a matter of importance if you were going on a journey, or hunting or fishing. The earliest English example is to be found on the Bayeux Tapestry ~ 1086. The church weathercock was the subject of a Saxon riddle & reminds us of Peter's denial of CHRIST ~ John 13:38. Banner-shaped vanes were commonly used on houses. These could be embellished with initials or a date. Fishes also appear ~ another Christian symbol & so do the foxes so often pursued in the hunting field. Dragons & other heraldic beasts will also be found among the galaxy of silhouettes that creaked away above our country houses. The device above shows how a dial on a house exterior could indicate the wind direction. Other versions had interior dials ~ there was once one in a Marlborough ~ Wilts ~ inn.

Simple bevel gears translate the horizontal movement of the vane into a vertical movement on the dial.

ESTATE TRANSPORT

The working estate needed
a variety of vehicles to carry out its different tasks.
In practical terms the hardest~worked vehicle was the
tip cart. This could be adapted by the addition of
harvest ladders for the more bulky lighter hay or
corn crops. Denser loads, like dung, could also be
carried & so could milk churns. Carts outnumbered
wagons because they were more adaptable. Wagons could
carry more than a cart but when fully loaded
needed at least two horses. Long~bodied carts
were also widely used for harvest work in hilly
places as they were easier to turn than a wagon.
Special carts were used to carry water which was
an essential task in days before a piped water
supply reached isolated farms.

A factory made tip-cart
with harvest ladders
added at front & rear.
The tip-up body
increased the cart's
usefulness.

Illustration from an
old catalogue.

A long-cart designed for harvest work. The side-ladders added to
the cart's capacity. An example from Devon.

This water cart has a galvanised
tank. The load was kept
low by the use of a ⊓
shaped axle. This
lowered the centre of
gravity & allowed the
vehicle to turn more
easily.
The wheels reveal
that it had a
military origin ~
probably c.1916.
It remained
in use until
the 1960s.!

CARRIAGES

Travelling was an important matter for those who lived in a country house. Any excursion needed the involvement of those who worked in the stables. A variety of vehicles had evolved to provide transport for the country gentleman & his family. Some were driven by the master or his wife ~ like the phaeton, gig or buggy. For family travel the private coach, handled by the coachman, was used. These were large & robust like stage coaches. When the family moved to its town house, or to a spa for a season, the servants were taken too ~ they rode outside! The hand-drawn carriage, used for the slow perambulation of the park, displays typical coach features.

This unusual vehicle was made to carry a wheelchair & allowed its occupant to drive.

ENTRANCE RAMP

MANY DIFFERENT VEHICLES WERE USED AROUND THE ESTATE. THE PHAETON WAS FOR PLEASURE DRIVING BUT THE WAGONETTE HAD A MORE PRACTICAL PURPOSE.

C. 1880 LADIES' PHAETON

C. 1890 GIG

C. 1900 DOG CART

C. 1900 WAGONETTE WITH SIX SEATS

C. 1870 FOUR-WHEELED DOG CART

C. 1890 STANHOPE GIG

FIREFIGHTING

FIRE was always a risk and its consequences held great terror in the days before there was a public fire brigade. The GREAT FIRE ~ 1666~ in London was followed by improvements in the technology of fire-fighting equipment. The first of these was the introduction of a mobile pump like the type made by Newsham in the mid-C18. A pump was not much use without a supply of water & a human chain of buckets had to be established to feed the pump's thirst. Water had to be placed in the tank (W) before it could be pumped into the hose~fixed at (H). Men stood at each side of the machine & vigorously pumped the handrail (R) up & down. There was a limit to the pressure obtained from a handpump. Late in Victoria's reign the steam pump was introduced. This also had a disadvantage ~ it would

FIREHOOK   USED FOR PULLING THATCH FROM BURNING BUILDINGS.

THE CORRIDOR ENGINE
FORCED A JET 50 FT.
IT COULD BE PLACED
UPSTAIRS. IN 1890
IT COST £6-10-0.

not operate until the boiler pressure had been raised. A cold steam engine was no use at all. Most of the hand engines were drawn by man or horse power. They were slow to travel distances, & that is why estates usually invested in their own engines. In large houses fire extinguishers were placed at strategic points. Some fires were caused by oil lamps & early chemical extinguishers were invented to combat them. In the battle against fire JOHN MORRIS & Sons, of Salford, manufactured a GRENADE. This 'being of the thinnest glass will break as easily as an egg, & can therefore be used by a child.' The user was advised to 'throw the grenades into the midst of the fire in quick succession until it extinguished, using considerable force to scatter the liquid.'

ABOVE · FIRE GRENADES
COST £2-00 PER DOZEN IN
THE 1890s.
LEFT · HORSEDRAWN
FIRE ENGINE ~ C.1890~.
THE WATER WAS PUMPED
MANUALLY LIKE THE
NEWSHAM ENGINE OPPOSITE.

109

ERDDIG~CLWYD: An octagonal dovecote in brick with a tiled roof, & four dormer windows. The lantern at the apex has an elegant vane.

STEWKLEY~BUCKS: This example has patterned brickwork. The lantern is missing but the vane is probably part of the original design.

DOVECOTES

Fresh meat was a rare commodity in the days before improved methods of animal husbandry allowed cattle to be overwintered. One mediaeval answer to this problem was the keeping of doves in DOVECOTES. The birds lived upon anyone's growing crops during the summertime & could be fed on corn during the winter. The privilege of keeping doves was restricted to the Lord of the Manor, or the clergy. They alone could enjoy pigeon pie when lesser inhabitants had at best salted beef or fish. Some dovecotes date from the time of Norman rule, but many were constructed in the C18 or later. These reflect the architectural fashions of the age, and like so many man-made objects they all possess unique individual characteristics. You will not find one design repeated in another place. There were some estates which had a matching pair of dovecotes but these are exceptions.

Older designs were often square in plan but the most useful arrangement was circular or octagonal. This allowed the use of a potence ~ a timber structure which supported ladders & could rotate. In this way it was easy for the keeper to reach any of the pigeon holes in the surrounding wall. During the C17 there were said to be some twenty-six thousand dovecotes in England.

KEY TO DIAGRAM ~

A~ The lantern which was the main entrance for the birds. B~ Lead flashing to make the roof watertight. C~ Dormer window to provide light. D~ Tie beam to support roof timbers. E~ Potence shaft with upper bearing housed in tie beam. F~ Diagonal braces to support ladder rests. G~ Ladder rests. H~ Ladders. J~ Stone base to support E. K~ Resting platform. L~ Landing ledges. M~ Nest holes. N~ String course to provide a rodent barrier. O~ Dripstone to deter rodents. P~ Dung from the birds was collected for tanners who used it to soften leather. Saltpetre, potassium nitrate, derived from pigeon droppings ~ & other animal waste ~ was an essential element in gunpowder manufacture.

Eating of doves' flesh is of force against the PLAGUE. They who make it their constant food are seldom seized by pestilential diseases. Others commend it against the PALSIE & TREMBLING. It is of great advantage to them that are dim-sighted. The flesh of young pigeons is restorative.

WILLUGHBY ~ 'PIGEONS' ~ C17

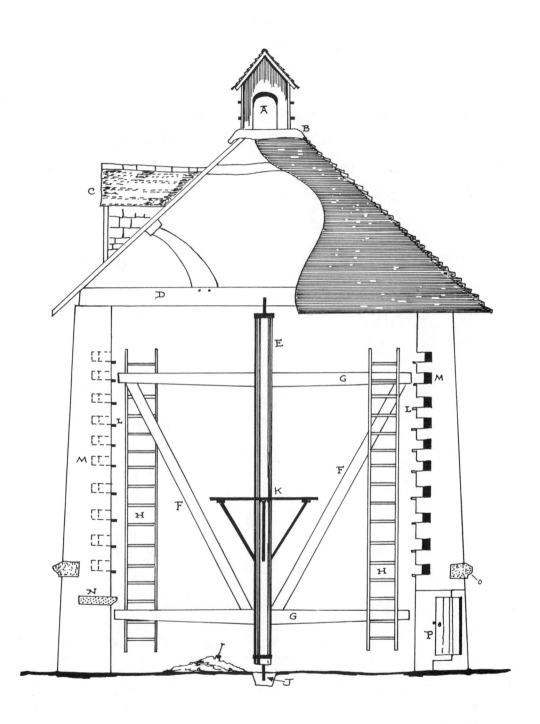

113

THE
TIMBER WAGON

In the C19 timber was still a very basic material with a place in so many aspects of life. Large estates had significant stands of timber, which were carefully husbanded by the agent. When timber was felled it had to be carried back to the estate timber yard. The timber wagon had the same structure as a traditional wagon ~ with a forecarriage which could turn & a long pole to link the hind axle to the front. Once felled timber would stand up to seven years stacked in the yard. There it could slowly weather & so would not warp when the carpenter came to work it.

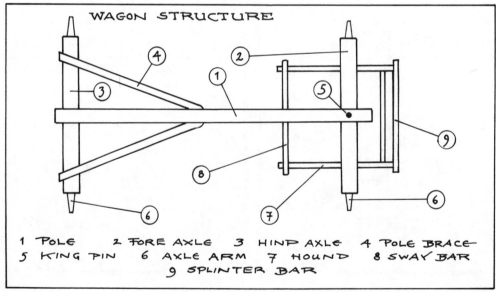

WAGON STRUCTURE

1 POLE   2 FORE AXLE   3 HIND AXLE   4 POLE BRACE
5 KING PIN   6 AXLE ARM   7 HOUND   8 SWAY BAR
9 SPLINTER BAR

CROSS-CUT SAW - USED TO DIVIDE A STOCK INTO A REQUIRED LENGTH

A lot of muscle power was needed to move a log from the ground onto the timber wagon. This was done inch by inch with sloping planks & long levers. To prevent the tree from rolling off, vertical poles (x) were slotted into the upper members ~ bolsters~ of both fore & hind carriages.

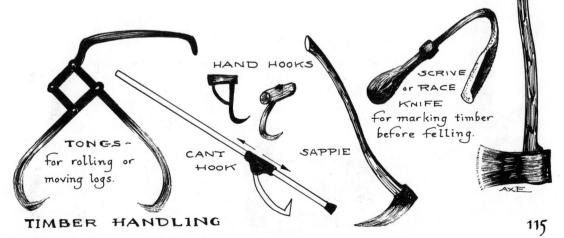

TONGS~ for rolling or moving logs.

HAND HOOKS

CANT HOOK

SAPPIE

SCRIVE or RACE KNIFE for marking timber before felling.

AXE

TIMBER HANDLING

115

TIMBER YARD

Until the advent of the steam powered circular saw all the trees were reduced to planks by a large handsaw operated by two men. The timber was rolled over a pit and made secure with timber dogs (x) that prevented any movement. It was the top sawyer's job to keep the cut straight. He stood on the trunk. The bottom sawyer in the pit made the cut on each downstroke & suffered the falling sawdust.

This method of sawing was slow. Some sawyers were itinerants who were paid by the number of feet sawn & were usually given an allowance of beer. As the sawing progressed the supports (b), wedges (c) & dogs (x) were adjusted to allow for the passage of the saw blade.

To make it easier to move heavy logs the workmen used a RING DOG to grip the log & roll it into the required position.

PIT SAW

116

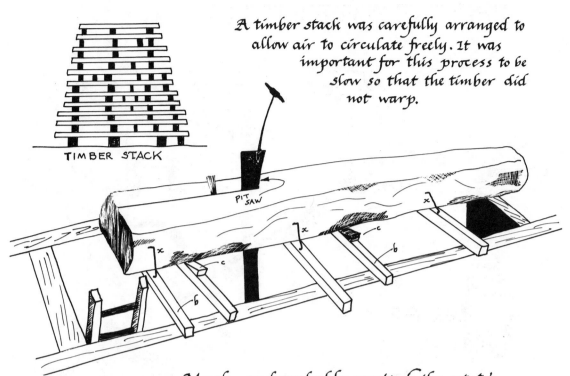

A timber stack was carefully arranged to allow air to circulate freely. It was important for this process to be slow so that the timber did not warp.

TIMBER STACK

PIT SAW

Much, and probably most, of the estate's timber production was used on the estate. Apart from repairs to farm buildings, cottages & the erection of new buildings; a great deal of the lighter timber was prepared for fencing. The natural curves of a tree were helpful to the woodman who was quick to see the shape of a cart's shafts in the growing timber.

TIMBER DOG

SLEDGE HAMMER

WEDGE

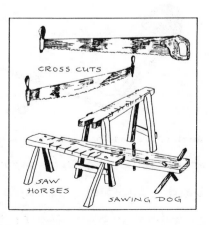

CROSS CUTS

SAW HORSES

SAWING DOG

THE CARPENTER

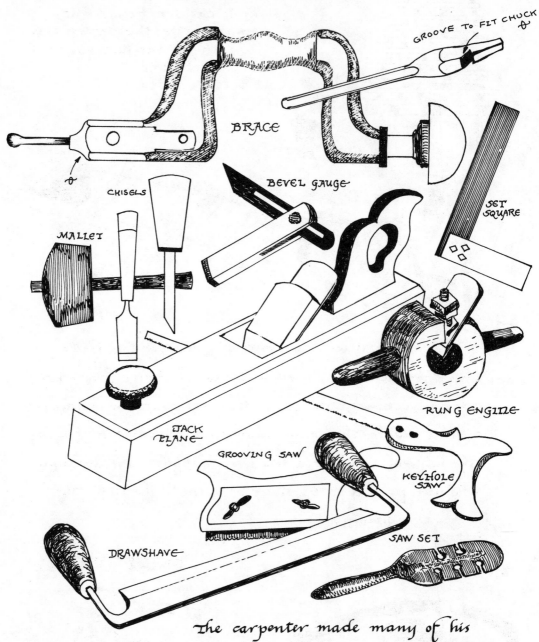

GROOVE TO FIT CHUCK

BRACE

BEVEL GAUGE

CHISELS

SET SQUARE

MALLET

RUNG ENGINE

JACK PLANE

GROOVING SAW

KEYHOLE SAW

DRAWSHAVE

SAW SET

The carpenter made many of his own tools with a little help from the blacksmith. The design of woodworking tools changed very little from the Roman era until C20. Many things used on the estate, by craftsmen & indoors, were made by the carpenter as the facing page shows.

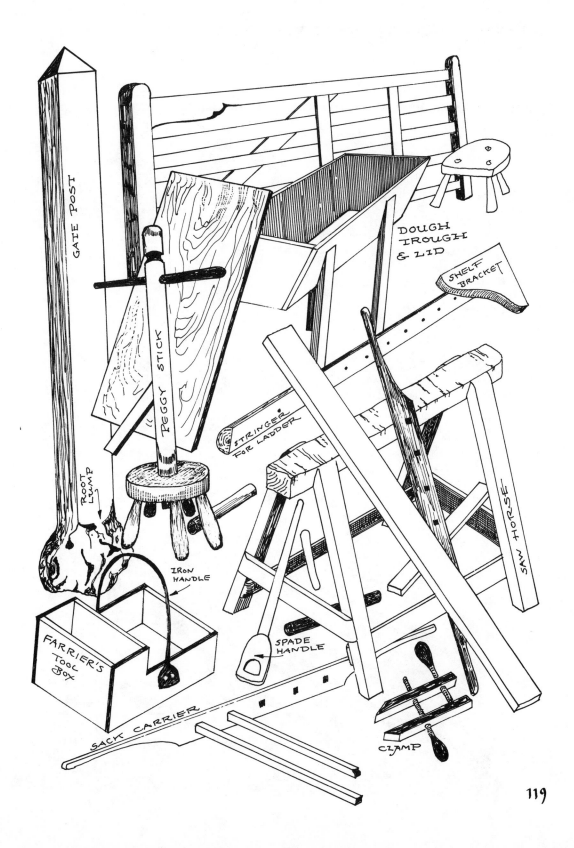

GATE POST

DOUGH TROUGH & LID

SHELF BRACKET

PEGGY STICK

STRINGER FOR LADDER

SAW HORSE

ROOT LUMP

IRON HANDLE

SPADE HANDLE

FARRIER'S TOOL BOX

SACK CARRIER

CLAMP

119

THE BLACKSMITH

The ANVIL was used for hammering hot iron especially when horses from the estate came for shoeing. Many tools had special functions & were made by the craftsman himself. An old-style leg vice was also a vital part of his gear.

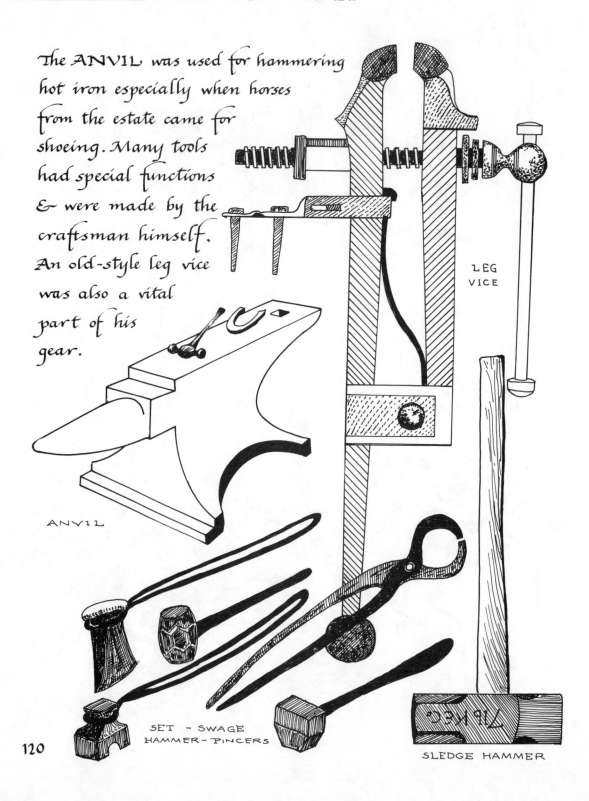

LEG VICE

ANVIL

SET - SWAGE
HAMMER - PINCERS

SLEDGE HAMMER

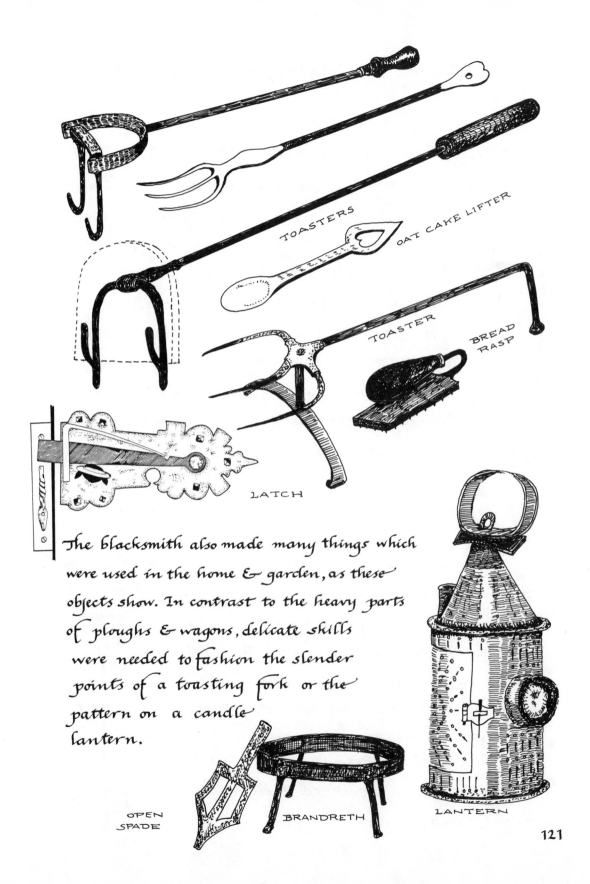

TOASTERS

OAT CAKE LIFTER

TOASTER

BREAD RASP

LATCH

The blacksmith also made many things which were used in the home & garden, as these objects show. In contrast to the heavy parts of ploughs & wagons, delicate skills were needed to fashion the slender points of a toasting fork or the pattern on a candle lantern.

OPEN SPADE

BRANDRETH

LANTERN

THE WHEELWRIGHT

Many of the carpenter's tools were commonly used by the wheelwright. There were also many special tools used specifically by those who made wheels for wagons & wheelbarrows. The preparation of the many timber parts which made up a wheel was a precise task & for this work the craftsman often used a wooden template. In horsedrawn days, before wagons were built in factories, there were no drawings to consult. Tradition, the craftsman's eye & a pattern were all that construction required. In common with many crafts, its tools were frequently home made~ like the traveller which measured the circumference of a tyre. Tools like the brace were often made with a fixed bit.

SAMPSON USED FOR PULLING STRAKE TYRES TOGETHER BEFORE NAILING.

This meant that a separate brace was needed for each size of hole to be bored. If a tool had to be made in metal then the blacksmith would make it to the wheelwright's specification. When a wheel had been made the final task was to shrink on the iron hoop tyre. At this stage the smith & the wheelwright often combined their skills at the tyring ring.

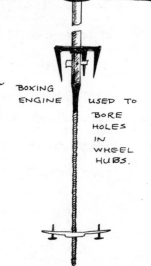

BOXING ENGINE USED TO BORE HOLES IN WHEEL HUBS.

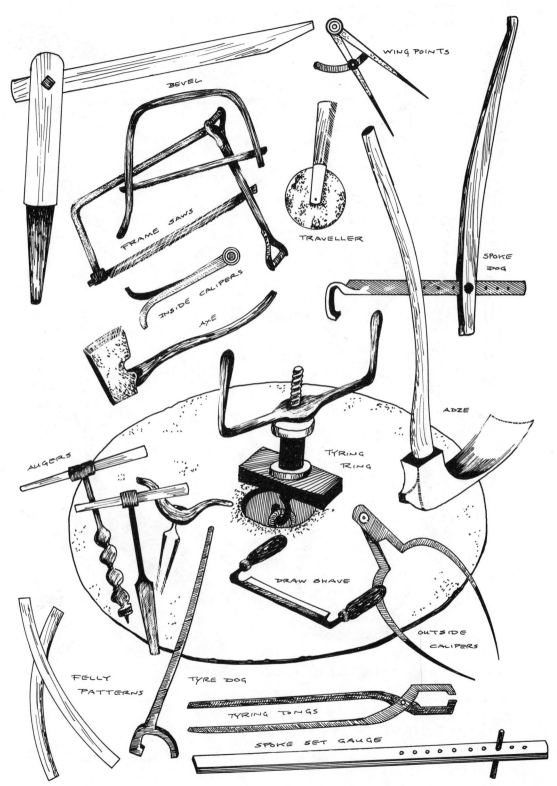

BEVEL

WING POINTS

FRAME SAWS

TRAVELLER

SPOKE DOG

INSIDE CALIPERS

AXE

ADZE

AUGERS

TYRING RING

DRAW SHAVE

OUTSIDE CALIPERS

FELLY PATTERNS

TYRE DOG

TYRING TONGS

SPOKE SET GAUGE

123

THE WHITESMITH

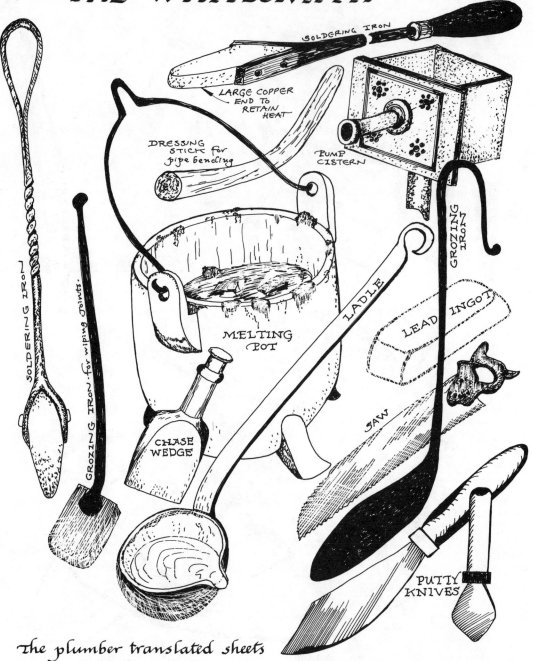

SOLDERING IRON

LARGE COPPER END TO RETAIN HEAT

DRESSING STICK for pipe bending

PUMP CISTERN

SOLDERING IRON

GROZING IRON for wiping joints.

MELTING POT

CHASE WEDGE

LADLE

LEAD INGOT

GROZING IRON

SAW

PUTTY KNIVES

The plumber translated sheets
and ingots of lead into useful objects. He made his pipes,
cisterns & spouts using very simple tools. Glazing was
also part of his craft when most windows had small
124 panes set in leadwork.

BRICKMAKING

Brickmaking was practised by a great number of estates. Brickearth was excavated in the winter months & left to mature in the frost. You can still see old kilns in what is now pastureland. Undulations

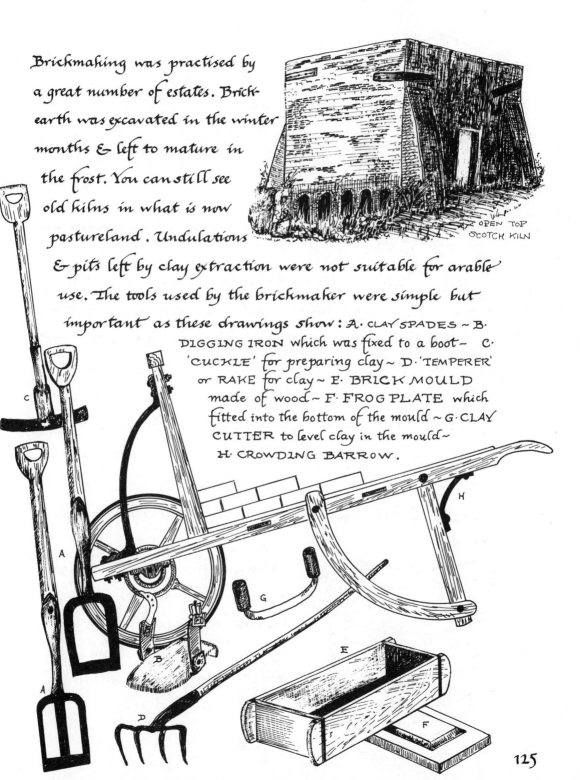

AN OPEN TOP SCOTCH KILN

& pits left by clay extraction were not suitable for arable use. The tools used by the brickmaker were simple but important as these drawings show: A. CLAY SPADES ~ B. DIGGING IRON which was fixed to a boot ~ C. 'CUCKLE' for preparing clay ~ D. 'TEMPERER' or RAKE for clay ~ E. BRICK MOULD made of wood ~ F. FROG PLATE which fitted into the bottom of the mould ~ G. CLAY CUTTER to level clay in the mould ~ H. CROWDING BARROW.

ICE HOUSES

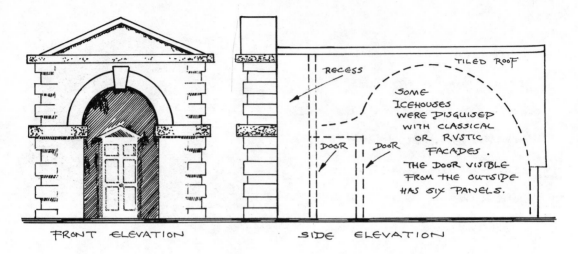

FRONT ELEVATION   SIDE ELEVATION

Within the side elevation: RECESS · TILED ROOF · SOME ICEHOUSES WERE DISGUISED WITH CLASSICAL OR RUSTIC FACADES. THE DOOR VISIBLE FROM THE OUTSIDE HAS SIX PANELS. · DOOR · DOOR

Refrigeration is taken for granted these days, but the business of making things cold was a different matter in the C18. Winters seem to have been more severe in that age, which was just as well for those workmen who had to cut ice blocks from the lakes. It was then barrowed to the ice house. These constructions were like icebergs, as the greater part of their structure was invisible. The cross-sectional view of a typical ice-house is shown opposite. It was about 25 ft. in depth & 12-15 ft in diameter. A drain was placed at the base so that the ice did not become waterlogged. Doors always faced north so that direct sunlight could not penetrate.

ICE BUCKET

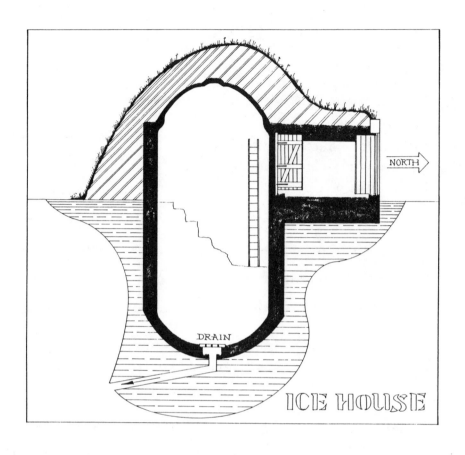

DRAIN

NORTH →

ICE HOUSE

There was always an outer & an inner door ~ sometimes two. Straw was placed between these doors to provide extra insulation. Trees were grown on or around the earth mound to give shade.

Ice houses placed in the parkland were disguised with classical or rustic exteriors. Ice was removed in summer & taken to the house for cooling wine etc.

ICE HOUSE STRUCTURE WITHOUT THE MOUND.

THE DECOY

Fresh meat could also be obtained during winter months from the Duck Decoy ~ an idea borrowed from Holland in the C16. A decoy pond had to be located in a quiet undisturbed place that was sheltered. To trap wildfowl you needed a PIPE covered

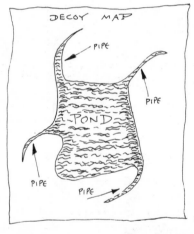

DECOY MAP

PIPE
PIPE
POND
PIPE
PIPE

by hoops which supported the netting. Each pipe was curved so that the end could not be seen from the entrance. As you progressed from the entrance the hoops became lower. The pond was in the care of a decoy-man ~ assisted by a dog ~ 'a piper'. Decoy ducks were half bred mallard. These birds were regularly fed & some, those without pinioned wings, could fly free to attract other birds to the decoy pond. Home bred birds were used to the decoy man & his piper. They would come when called to be fed, & would readily enter the pipe to collect

CROSS SECTION OF
A PIPE · SHOWING
DIMINISHING HEIGHT · NOT TO SCALE

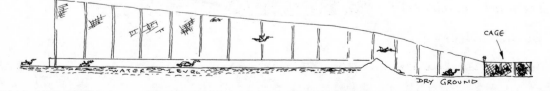

WATER LEVEL

CAGE

DRY GROUND

grain thrown over the 7ft. high straw screens. The wild birds followed. Once the wild duck were in the pipe the dog was signalled to jump a low screen ∅~18"high~ which linked most of the screens. The dog's appearance excited   the birds' curiosity which   increased when the dog   jumped back again

& was lost

to sight.

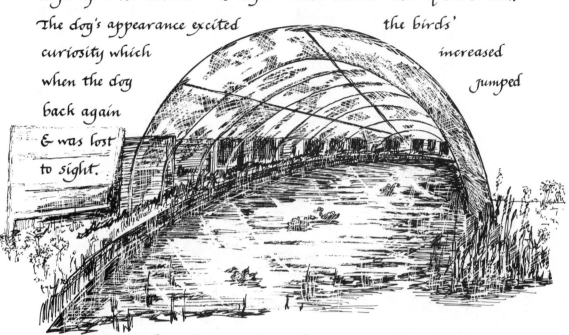

Then they moved up the pipe to investigate. As soon as this happened the decoy man showed himself between the screens. The wild birds took fright & flew further into the curving pipe. Of course the home bred birds did not, but returned to the pond. Gradually the trapped birds were worked towards the pipe's end. When they were within the trap net (Y) they could be removed for the cook's use.

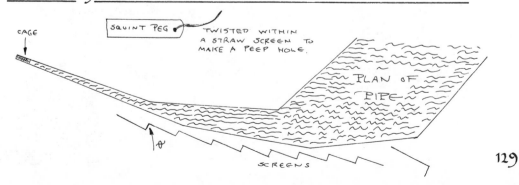

CAGE

SQUINT PEG   TWISTED WITHIN A STRAW SCREEN TO MAKE A PEEP HOLE.

PLAN OF PIPE

∅

SCREENS

129

SHOOTING

CARTRIDGE BELT

GAME CARRIER

GUN CASE

GAME JAG

BEWARE
MANTRAPS &
SPRING GUNS
are set in these woods

'Whosoever shall set or place any Spring Gun, Man Trap or other Engine calculated to destroy Human Life or inflict grevious bodily Harm with the intent that the same... may inflict Harm upon a Trespasser or other Person coming in contact therewith, shall be guilty of a Misdemeanour, & being convicted thereof shall be liable... to be kept in Penal Servitude for the term of Three Years.'

SPRING GUNS were devised c.1817 & they became illegal, along with Mantraps, by the Act of 1861. [24/25 VICTORIA CAP. 100]

SHOOTING STICK

GUN CASES

130

1820

Until the 1860s the flintlock muzzle-
loader was the standard type of sporting gun.
It was heavy & slow to load, & there was some
delay between the trigger being pulled & the
shot leaving the muzzle, which meant the target
had to be followed for some time. It was superseded
by the cartridge-firing breechloader. At first the
cartridges were pin-fire, set off by a projecting
pin being forced down by a hammer. The cartridge
as we know it today was then introduced, together
with the snap action to open & close the gun.
The hammerless gun appeared in the late 1870s.
The last refinement was the automatic ejector
mechanism, which actually propelled the used
cartridge out of the barrel, & so speeded up
reloading.

1884

Another way of keeping the house larder stocked with suitable birds involved the WILDFOWLER. He could work for six months of the year, prior to the Wild Birds Protection Act - 1880, & operated by night & day. The immense PUNT GUN which was fixed to the slender punt was upwards of 8ft in length & had a bore of 1¼ inches. These guns used about 2½ ozs. of powder & a pound of shot at each firing! Birds were approached stealthily by using the wind & the CREEPING STICKS, that were fixed to strings to prevent them being lost. On frozen lakes the hunter fixed his gun to a sledge ~ guided over the ice by shorter creeping sticks shown below.

Few records exist to show how many birds were shot but one known fowler averaged more than 300 a season for 17 years ~ i.e. a total bag of more than 5000.

POACHERS

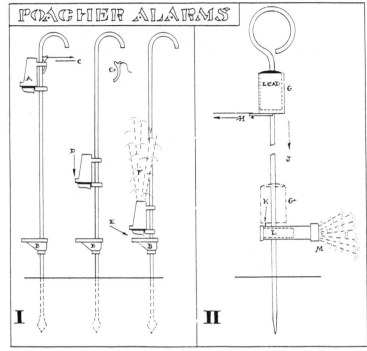

POACHER ALARMS

I

II

The gamekeepers were constantly aware of the need to deter poachers. In the early years of the C19 poacher alarms were made which worked from a trip wire. Two designs are shown. They worked in the following way. I~ The iron rod was pushed into the ground. A crescent-shaped catch ·C· was attached to the top of the rod & from it stretched the trip wire. Within the canister ·A· a cartridge was placed. If an intruder moved the tripwire the catch ·C· was released. Canister ·A· then fell downwards ·→D· & struck the anvil ·B·. The force of the fall discharged the cartridge·F. The older version II~ has a rim-fire cartridge ·L·. Its trip wire ·H· works in the same way as I. This releases the weight ·G· which falls ·→J· until it stops at ·G+·. The pin of the rim-fire cartridge ·K· is pushed inwards and the alarm ·M· is given. Alarm signals were audible over considerable distances and gamekeepers had to be ready to give chase at a moment's notice.

THE GAMEKEEPER

Caring for & rearing game birds needed tranquillity.
Keepers dwelt in the quiet parts of the estate
where they could pursue their craft undisturbed.
The inscription below provides a glimpse of the
gamekeeper's demanding work ~ it commemorates
Robert Mossendew, keeper to the Ashby family,
who died in 1744. His memorial can still be seen
on an exterior north wall, at Harefield church,
Uxbridge, Middx.

'In frost & snow, thro' hail & rain
He scour'd the woods, & trudg'd the plain;
The steady pointer leads the way,
Stands at the scent, then springs the prey;
The timorous birds from stubble rise,
With pinions stretch'd divide the skies;
The scattered lead pursues the sight
And death in thunder stops their flight;
His spaniel, of true English kind,
With gratitude inflames his mind;
This servant in an honest way,
In all his actions copied Tray.'

A GAMEKEEPER'S MEMORIAL FROM THE
NORTH. IT SHOWS SOME OF HIS EQUIPMENT,
A GUNDOG AND A GAMEBIRD.

GATES & LODGES

THE PUBLIC face of a house was always important. Apart from the frontage of the house itself great attention was paid to the entrance, which was often some distance away. This had to make a public statement about the owner's status. Many grand entrances were exalted gateposts fashioned by masons. The two spheres on the example shown above are reminders of the severed heads feudal lords used to adorn their gateways & proclaim their absolute authority. By the C18 the spheres sometimes were replaced by pineapples ~ a symbol of hospitality. Earlier GATEHOUSES performed two functions ~ they established status & safety. Their origins lie in the barbicans of mediaeval towns & castles. In turbulent times owners often erected them & they provided living space for a watchful retainer. Each night the gates were closed to secure the safety of animals & humans within.

CHIPPING CAMPDEN.
GLOS.

By the C18 see-through gateways began to replace the solid secretive boundaries of earlier days. The introduction of elaborate ironwork screens & gates still spoke of power & influence but they allowed the traveller to glimpse the park within & sometimes the house itself. The gateway was the overture for the forthcoming drama.

PEPPERPOTS · GT. HAMPDEN. BUCKS.

ESTATES had several entrances and lesser ones still had to establish authority, but they did not require such a great degree of splendour. The more modest entrance shown above guarded a vista but it was not a principal point of access. The gateposts however with their wooden 'heads' still echo a mediaeval idea. Living in such a divided house must have posed problems for the gate-keeper. Once a family of ten was reared in these two 'pepperpots'. By the C19 ideas of rustic charm began to engage the interest of gentlemen & 'cottages ornées' like this one began to proclaim to the world that the owner was in step with Picturesque fashion.

RUSTIC COTTAGE

POSTSCRIPT

The Country House was at its zenith in the later Georgian period. Under Victoria it became overblown. The massive wealth, derived from industry, allowed the Mister Gradgrinds of this new world to indulge their own self-aggrandisement. Classical styles in architecture gave way to Gothic Revival or Tudorbethan. The Industrial Revolution that allowed such extravagance also created changes which determined its decline. Demand for cheap food from urban populations brought about the repeal of the despised Corn Laws in the 1840s. When the development of the railroads in N. America opened up the prairies British agriculture suffered a long decline. This depression reduced the landed aristocracy's & gentry's rent income in a significant manner from the 1870s.

Lloyd George's Death Duties & Surtax in 1909 added to the difficulties of the great estates. County Councils, post 1888, also diminished the aristocracy's powers. The House of Lords' loss of its power to veto legislation, & the extension of the franchise changed the political equation. New Country Houses did appear however, & architects like Sir Edwin Lutyens introduced a distinctive neo-Georgianism into the countryside. Even in 1939 there were still more than a million domestic servants at work.

Since 1945 some four hundred country houses have been demolished. A postwar upturn in farming profits & the rise in the value of land, old masters & antiques has nevertheless helped the remaining estates to survive. Economic considerations have encouraged owners to follow the path blazed by The National Trust, & hundreds of estates remain intact partly as a consequence of their paying visitors.

The final demise of the live-in domestic servant came about in the 1960s, when manual labour was replaced by machines to launder & clean, & cook automatically. The function of the kitchen also changed & it became a focus for living instead of an element of service. Its status was raised to that of an alternative drawing room.

Stable blocks were converted to flats, redundant gatehouses, lodges & estate cottages were often sold off. When tenancies fell in some farmhouses were also disposed of to create working capital for the development of new enterprises. The estate shoot too began to operate on a commercial basis in order to generate revenue.

BOOT JACK

The new country houses still being built do not need a large servants' wing. Late C20 architects can therefore achieve a balanced composition much more easily.

When we consider the objects which surrounded this now lost way of life we should look beyond their function & ask ourselves questions about those who made them & those who used them in their daily lives. The Sheraton sideboard & the battered watering can may each have a story to tell.

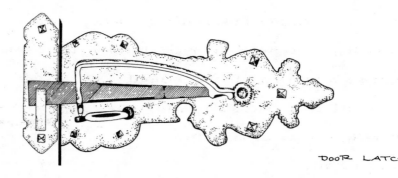

DOOR LATCH

ACKNOWLEDGEMENTS

The author wishes to acknowledge the help he has received from the following institutions & individuals:- Bucks. County Museum; The Cotswold Collection, Northleach, Glos.; Holker Hall, Cumbria; Holst's House, Cheltenham, Glos.; Museum of Lakeland Life & Industry, Kendal; The National Trust ~ Calke Abbey; Sulgrave Manor; The Tradescant Trust; Yr Ymddiriedolaeth Genedlaethol ~ Erddig; Thora Anstee; Iris Greenway; Henry North; Mr. & Mrs. John G. Sims; John Cox; Rosemary Nicholson; John Anstee; J.R. Chichester-Constable; K. Usher; R. Dillon; Martin Cyro-Smith; George Hulbert; Victoria Slowe; Christopher Butler. & Roger Hudson ~ who generously contributed his special knowledge.

~PLACES TO VISIT~

There are hundreds of country houses which can be visited. The list below is a small selection of the visible treasures still accessible to those who wish to explore an important part of the nation's heritage. Details of opening times are subject to change & for up-to-date information on all houses open to the public the reader is directed to the current edition of 'HISTORIC HOUSES CASTLES & GARDENS in GREAT BRITAIN & IRELAND', British Leisure Publications. A copy of this annual publication will be found in the reference section of most libraries. Its entries describe the special features of each house.

Belvoir Castle, Grantham, Leics.

Boughton Monchelsea Place, Maidstone, Kent.

Bowood, Calne, Wilts.

Broughton Castle, Banbury, Oxon.

Burghley House, Stamford, Lincs.

Burton Constable Hall, Hull, North Humberside.

Calke Abbey, Ticknall, Derbys.

Claverton Manor, Bath, Avon.

Chatsworth, Bakewell, Derbys.

East Riddesden Hall, Keighly, W.Yks.

Erddig, Wrexham, Clwyd.

Felbrigg Hall, Cromer, Norfolk.

Greys Court, Henley-on-Thames, Oxon.

Hergest Croft Gardens, Kington, Heref.

Holker Hall, Cark-in-Cartmel, Cumbria.

Holst's House, Cheltenham, Glos.

Houghton Lodge, Stockbridge, Hants.

Lanhydrock, Bodmin, Cornwall.

The Lawns, Broseley, Much Wenlock, Salop.

Levens Hall, Kendal, Cumbria.

Longleat House, Warminster, Wilts.

Mary Arden's House, Wilmcote, Warw.

Michelham Priory, Hailsham, Sussex.

National Garden Museum, Lambeth, London.

Newick Park, Lewes, Sussex.

Normanby Park, Scunthorpe, Humberside.

Number One, Royal Crescent, Bath, Avon.

The Old Hall, Gainsborough, Lincs.

Over Peover, Knutsford, Cheshire.

Peckover House, Wisbech, Cambs.

Poundisford Park, Pitminster, Taunton, Som.

Raby Castle, Staindrop, Co. Durham.

Rousham House, Steeple Aston, Oxon.

Saltram House, Plymouth, Devon.

Shugborough, Stafford, Staffs.

Somerleyton Hall, Lowestoft, Suff.

Stowe, Buckingham, Bucks.

Sulgrave Manor, Brackley, N.hants.

The Swiss Garden, Old Warden, Beds.

Trerice, St. Newlyn East, Cornwall.

Wightwick Manor, Wolverhampton, West Midlands.

INDEX

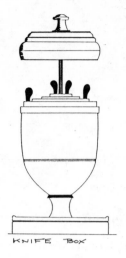

KNIFE BOX

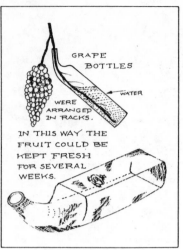

GRAPE BOTTLES

WATER

WERE ARRANGED IN RACKS.

IN THIS WAY THE FRUIT COULD BE KEPT FRESH FOR SEVERAL WEEKS.

HIGH CHAIR

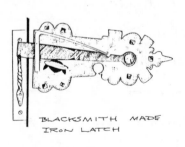

BLACKSMITH MADE IRON LATCH

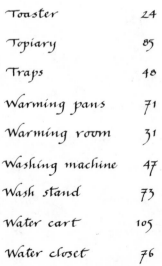